Introducing Narrative Therapy

A collection of practice-based writings

collected by

Cheryl White & David Denborough

DULWICH CENTRE PUBLICATIONS

ADELAIDE
SOUTH AUSTRALIA

Copyright © 1998 *by* Dulwich Centre Publications
ISBN 0 9586678 4 5

published by
Dulwich Centre Publications
Hutt St PO Box 7192
Adelaide, South Australia 5000
phone (61-8) 8223 3966 fax (61-8) 8232 4441

printed & manufactured in Australia by:
Graphic Print Group, Richmond, South Australia

100% recycled
paper

cover artwork by: Susy Stiles, Torrensville, South Australia
typeset, layout & design by: Jane Hales, Melrose Pk, South Australia

Contents

Contents (cont'd)

Introduction

The process of putting together this book has been invigorating. It has been just lovely to gather together this collection of writings by a diversity of authors, and to realise the ripples and new conversations that these writings have generated over the past few years.

We are consistently asked by people attending training, or at workshops and conferences, what we'd recommend as an introduction to narrative ideas and ways of working. Now, when we are asked this question, we'll be able to suggest this book!

Within it we have gathered together a diversity of accessible, engaging, practice-based papers, which all received enthusiastic feedback when they were first published. For therapists, community workers, or others who are wanting to understand more about narrative therapy and the different ways in which people are exploring and experimenting with narrative ways of working, this book offers a thorough and easy-to-read introduction.

The range of experiences and work with individuals, groups, and communities described in the following pages, is wonderfully diverse. From the knowledges of skills of the Power To Our Journeys group who document their journey in reclaiming their lives from the voices and visions of what is often called schizophrenia; to work with women about the effects of sexual abuse and anorexia nervosa; to the villages of Malawi, Africa, in which conversations are taking place with Mr AIDS and Mrs CARE; to research with young people on the experiences of self-abuse; to work by and with Indigenous Australians on issues of diabetes and grief; to invitations to 'say hullo again' to loved ones who have died; to stories of work with people whose lives are more 'weirdly-abled' than others; to narrative-based adventure camps with young people; this collection of papers, we hope, will challenge and inspire.

We look forward to hearing your feedback, to witnessing the further ripples of this work.

<table>
<tr><td>**Cheryl White**</td><td>**David Denborough**</td></tr>
<tr><td>Editor</td><td>Staff writer</td></tr>
<tr><td>Dulwich Centre Publications</td><td>Dulwich Centre Publications</td></tr>
</table>

PART I

Introducing
the
ideas

1

Companions on a Journey[1]

The work of the Dulwich Centre Community Mental Health Project

The Dulwich Centre Community Mental Health Project was established in July 1992 as an attempt to meet the needs of people with diagnosed psychiatric disorders who were considered to be 'chronically' mentally ill, and who were looking for assistance over and above that available from the state-run psychiatric services.

In 1997 the history of the project, the experiences of community members (those people with psychiatric diagnoses who joined the project as a result of their histories of involvement with psychiatric services), as well as the experiences of team members (community support workers, therapists, and the project team co-ordinator), were recorded in 'Companions on a Journey: An exploration of an alternative community mental health project' (*Dulwich Centre Newsletter,* 1997 No.1).

Six years after it began, the Dulwich Centre Community Mental Health Project is now in a state of transition. The following extract from 'Companions on a Journey' is included here as it clearly outlines various aspects of narrative ways of working.

The Community Mental Health Project is based on narrative ways of working that challenge dominant ways of understanding mental illness. They do not locate the problem in the person but also look at the context, at society as a whole, and the impact that various aspects of our culture has upon us as individuals. This way of understanding and working reduces the feeling of craziness and isolation. It allows you to regain your sense of being an intelligent person. (community member)

The Dulwich Centre Community Mental Health Project starts from the premise that the job of the counsellor/community worker is to help people identify what they want in their own lives, and to reconnect with their own knowledges and skills. In order to enable this, a consistent way of working flows throughout the project, from individual counselling sessions to community work, informing conversations and the ways in which interactions are understood. This way of working has been described elsewhere as 'narrative ways of working' (see White & Epston 1990).

This section of the newsletter explores the work of the Community Mental Health Project and the 'narrative ways of working' informing it. It is arranged under the following headings:

(i)   How the stories of our lives shape our lives

(ii)   Externalizing conversations

(iii)   Historical explorations and the creation of new stories

(iv)   Honouring everyday actions of resistance

(v)   Documenting new stories

(vi)   Rituals - markers on a path

(vii)   Community creation of new stories

(viii) Naming injustice - exploring relations of power

(ix)   Questioning culture

(x)   Acknowledging the political nature of the work

(xi)   Acknowledging the ways in which the work is mutually enriching

(i) How the stories of our lives shape our lives

Narrative ways of working are based on the idea that people's lives and relationships are shaped by the 'stories' which individuals and communities of people develop in order to give meaning to their experiences. These 'narratives of meaning' do not simply reflect or represent our lives - they actually shape and constitute our lives.

When people experience hardship within our culture there are many invitations for them to see themselves as the problem, as deficient in some way, and to take on a dominant story about themselves as a 'failure' or being 'to blame'. The dominant culture encourages people to think of problems as purely personal, for which we as individuals are fully responsible, and so, when a person experiences problems this is often taken as a negative reflection on their character, nature and worth. 'The person' and 'the problem' come to be seen as one and the same. This can result in people feeling helpless to take action, or can restrict them to action that reinforces the problem. If you see yourself as the problem there's not much you can do except maybe act against yourself.

(ii) Externalizing conversations

The Community Mental Health Project, in all of its separate but related spheres, uses ways of talking about problems, known as 'externalizing conversations'. Externalizing practices involve a refusal to see problems as internal to people. The person is not the problem, the problem is the problem. 'Externalizing conversations' are conversations that create space for people to see themselves as separate from the problems that are affecting their lives. Once a problem is seen as separate from the identity of a person, this person is then in a position to take new action. S/he has the opportunity to resist or protest the problem, and/or renegotiate the relationship with the problem in other ways (see White & Epston 1990).

The Project has been created to assist people who have been recipients of mainstream psychiatric services due to their experiences of what others refer to as the auditory or visual hallucinations of schizophrenia. The community members prefer to describe these experiences as 'voices' and 'visions'. As the Community Mental Health Project is committed to recognising the reality of the experiences of community members, it therefore acknowledges the reality of the voices. As community members describe, the ways in which language is used is an important issue:

> *Everyday words don't stigmatise. I have found it helpful to change the diagnosis into words that everyone can understand. When I was understanding my life through the words of the diagnosis I could only do what the language of the psychiatrist told me to do - take my tablets. The diagnosis was enveloping. By putting the diagnosis into everyday words I can do other things to respond - for example tone down the effects of certain voices by laying down or listening to music.* (community member)

In all spheres of the project externalizing conversations enable community members to expose the effects and tactics of the 'voices' and 'visions' and create the possibility of changing their relationship with them. Many of the voices that community members experience speak in controlling and dominating ways and they make powerful authoritative claims about community members' lives and identities. Assisting community members to revise their relationships with the troublesome voices plays a very significant part in the interactions within the Project. The successful revision of this relationship invariably has a powerful effect on the quality of community members' lives and plays a considerable role in reducing the vulnerability to relapse. (For a detailed exploration of the use of narrative ways of working with psychotic experience see 'Psychotic Experience and Discourse' an interview with Michael White by Ken Stewart, in White 1995).

> *Being able to talk about the voices, what they are saying and what they are getting up to has been a huge thing. It has brought many changes. Up until my involvement in the project I had to keep quiet about the voices. I'd feared that if I told people about the voices, especially within the mainstream psychiatric services, then I'd have been labelled as being crazy. So I kept quiet. But being quiet forced me into playing along with power games set by the established mental health systems and this was not very healing. Having to play these games put me under lots of strain. I had to be constantly on my toes and it was quite exhausting.*
>
> *It was also really hard to keep quiet because the voices dominated my thinking. Some of the voices were really unkind and I had nobody to talk with about them. I felt very lonely and at times very frightened. Since being*

a part of the project, and being able to talk about the voices, there are now kind voices which help me. I'm no longer isolated with this secret but am able to talk about the voices and know that I am respected and my experiences acknowledged. This has made a huge difference to me. I feel I am a capable and worthwhile person and I no longer fear that I might possibly be going crazy. (community member)

Contexts are therefore created in which the tactics of the voices and the desires they have for community members' lives can be openly discussed. As well as creating the possibility for a revision of the community members' relationships with the troublesome voices, in some instances this also allows community members to enlist the support of friendly voices. And, importantly, it opens the possibility for honest relationships of support with other people.

Whilst I had to keep the voices a secret I was trapped in my house and my life was dictated by the voices. It used to be scary being so alone, especially when the voices troubled me and had me doubting myself. When I couldn't talk about the voices I didn't know whether what they were saying was true or not, whereas now I can discuss things and get a different perspective on issues. I am able to. listen to my own thoughts more and trust them. (community member)

Once the voices have been externalized they can no longer speak with the same absolute authority over a person's life. This creates the possibility for respectful relations with other people in which the community members' experiences of the voices and visions are openly acknowledged. Conversations can take place that explore the histories of the voices' influence on community members' lives and the ways in which their influence has been resisted.

(iii) Historical explorations and the creation of new stories

We share quite in-depth conversations that expose the histories of the voices, their current tactics, their effects and the ways in which I am able to resist them. (community member)

The Community Mental Health Project has found that exploring the history of the influence of the voices, and the histories of negative stories that community members have about their own identities, creates the possibility for different ways of thinking and action. Community members have often been recruited into powerfully negative stories about themselves and their lives. Through exploring how they have been recruited into thinking certain ideas about themselves, and who coached them into these views of their identity, they are able to trace the ways in which their identities have been constructed over time. These conversations can also open the possibility of seeing how particular ideas about identity can be imposed by others who have power over a person's life. Community members have commented that when they are able to see that their ideas about themselves actually have a history, it becomes easier to question them. It also becomes easier to identify the real effects that these ideas are having on their lives.

A second very important result of this process of historical exploration is that community members are able to identify times in their lives when they have acted in ways that do not fit with their negative views of themselves. Dominant stories of identity are very powerful, and tend to obscure actions which do not fit with them. The dominant story directs attention away from these 'exceptions' and prevents them from being recognised. The Project is interested in how community members can be assisted to pay attention to these 'exceptions' and use them as a gateway to the exploration of alternative knowledges of life and identity. These 'exceptions', both historical and current, are used to create new, preferred stories of identity by which to live.

Through externalizing the 'voices' and 'visions', and building upon exceptions in their lives, a context is created in which community members can rename the dominant story of their lives as one about survival, courage and active resistance.

(iv) Honouring everyday actions of resistance

The times we [community members and community support workers] *spend together are not just 'nice' times. They are times of very well thought out work - work that involves reclaiming our lives from the voices. Our times together often involve conversations that expose the tactics of the voices and highlight how we are resisting them. We also share times that physically challenge the voices. For example, the voices constantly demand that I don't go out, that I stay inside. To successfully do the opposite is therefore a powerful event. Together we may go for a walk on the beach. It is a walk on the beach in the knowledge that we are acting in solidarity against the voices. It's not just like two people getting together and going for a walk - even though that is all that people looking on would see. It is different because together we have a joint analysis of the situation and of how our actions together are contributing to changing my relationship with the voices and with life. The times shared together are like little treasures to hang hope onto and to build upon.* (community member)

In this way there is a context or meaning within which every conversation and every shared action takes place. Externalizing conversations often begin in therapeutic contexts and are then kept alive in the relationships between community members and community support workers throughout everyday conversations and events. The conversations and actions shared are reflected upon constantly as examples of further steps taken to reclaim lives from the influences of the voices. With each meeting, the new preferred stories of identity are further developed and at regular intervals ways are found to honour the steps which have been taken.

(v) Documenting new stories

We write documents up together. Writing the documents is just fantastic because then I've got something real in my hand to reinforce the work we've been doing. I like to focus on positive things. The last document I wrote was on the good things in my life. 'Five quiet days' was the name I gave to one of my documents to celebrate that I'd had five quiet days. The document listed how this could have happened and why this came about. I document all the strategies I've used in my life. (community member)

To strengthen and support new stories of identity community members record in written documents the ways they are standing up to the effects of the voices and visions. These documents are sometimes written in collaboration with therapists and community support workers while at other times community members write them for and with each other. These documents of people's own knowledges and skills have many purposes. Some community members carry the documents with them at all times so they are constantly available to be consulted: *They really give me courage to carry on. They give me something to hang hope onto. They are affirming and supportive.* (community member) For others these documents are seen as 'passports' which can assist them through crisis times. Importantly, documents of knowledges are often shared with others who may also find them useful and in this way a sense of solidarity and community is built upon.

(vi) Rituals - markers on a path

We create rituals. They are like markers - points of reference to acknowledge the journey. To honour how far we have come. It's like saying 'let's stop and look at the scenery before we move on to this new part'. It's so important. In all political struggles we need to see where we have come from and to honour this. (community member)

Moving from dominant stories about one's life to preferred stories is like making a journey from one identity to another. Creating markers on this journey can play an important role in enabling people to move forward in their lives, as described by a community member:

Rituals have been a powerful part of building community and celebrating events for us. As a farewell to my life on workers' compensation, we had a ritual at a property just out of the city in the hills. Throughout the time I had been on workers' compensation I had a huge file. So we planted trees to replenish the earth for all the paper that had been used on my case. We also planted some trees for the koalas in order to replace the trees that had been wasted on all the paperwork. Then we had a bonfire and I burnt my rehab file! It was a great thing to do. We have lots of celebrations whenever we meet.

It is important, I think, to create rituals that are full of love, that come from the heart and that lend support. These rituals are really important for me because they are a part of creating my new life in which there are happy times. We use rituals to mark the end of a horrible time and the beginning of hopefully a good time. To create meaningful rituals also means that everyone comes together, we get to see each other and share a warm-hearted event. This Christmas, one of the project team members came and brought a parcel of sparklers and candles for each of us. On New Year's Eve I lit one of the candles and one of the sparklers, you know, just on my own. Through ritual we renew our strength and build on friendships. (community member)

Within the Community Mental Health Project the use of rituals generates communities which in turn reflect and build upon preferred stories of identity.

(vii) Community creation of new stories

An important part of our work is the constant building of communities. All of the people within the project become involved in the identification of community, of other people in the community who can stand with people, literally or in spirit. (project team member)

If people are engaged in a project of challenging the dominant meanings of their lives, and creating alternative, preferred stories, then the participation of others in the creation and reflection of these stories is very important. The Project places a great deal of importance on finding ways in which other people and broader audiences can be invited to play a part in co-authoring, authenticating and strengthening the preferred stories of community members.

It is great having people on my side, you know, who present a different picture to what the voices are presenting. The voices always present the facts in a negative way. They distort life. It is fantastic to have a team which reflects on things in a different light, in the proper light. It is really fantastic to have a positive energy. (community member)

The identification of community often involves finding ways in which community members can 'carry community' with them in their everyday lives.

Sometimes when I am out in the world I get very scared. When I am on a train for example. But now I can close my eyes and think about the team and the Power to Our Journeys people. I can imagine us all together and the fear becomes less. Other people do it so easy, you know, they go out in the morning and can easily make a telephone call or spend five minutes on the telephone. They are not easy things for everyone. But as time passes within the project it gets easier. I feel a togetherness now that is just beautiful. I imagine us all. I gather our energy. I have you all with me as I step out into the world or even as I remember things from the past. It gives me extra strength. (community member)

Building a sense of community also involves finding ways of linking the lives of people in the project to the lives of others whom they may never have met.

One aspect of building communities involves finding ways of documenting the knowledges and skills of the community members and, with their permission, sharing some of the stories of their lives, their rich know-how, with others. Bringing back to the group the responses of these other people, these outsider witnesses, is often very powerful. In this way the stories of their lives are experienced as linked to the stories of the lives of others around shared themes, purposes and commitments. This process of telling and re-telling, and linking people's stories to the stories of the lives of others around shared themes, generates new options for action for community members. The process contributes to rich descriptions of their lives and is actually shaping of their lives. Community building and linking, telling and re-telling is a powerfully creative activity in the formation of lives. (project team member)

This process also occurs when project team members use the documents of community members in their work with others in different contexts.

When project team members in their work with other people use our documents and the knowledge we have gained about the voices and ways of resisting their influence on our lives it is really empowering. It is inspiring to know that we are indirectly helping other people. It brings a broader sense of solidarity. And when their feedback comes back to us then not only are we offering solidarity to them, but they are offering it back to us. We talk about this process as currents or ripples that are always flowing back and forth through this work. (community member)

Community members and project team members also talk about a further sense of community or a sense of solidarity with those people and communities who are challenging oppression and working for justice.

We have a saying in one of our documents: 'We are as strong as the ocean and as intelligent as the dolphins. We can withstand the destructiveness of the voices with intelligence and compassion.' This evokes for us a broader sense of solidarity with all the forces for life. (community member)

(viii) Naming injustice - exploring relations of power

We all come to the project with different perspectives on the politics of analysing and dealing with the voices, but I think I can safely say that we have a common bond. We all find it really useful to say that we are united together against the injustice of the voices. For myself, I have found it almost like a watershed, a revelation, to view the voices and deal with the voices as a political campaign. This is just my personal view which is informed by my past experience as a political activist. But I believe each one of us is a political activist in our own way because we each stand up to the injustice of the voices. For me anyway the bad voices are patriarchal, they oppress me, they want to keep my life limited. I feel like I run a political campaign against the injustice of the voices on a day-by-day, hour-by-hour, minute-by-minute basis with the goal being to get back my life or to have a life. I think that the political nature of the work is worth acknowledging. (community member)

The Community Mental Health Project is guided by the view that our individual stories and understandings of our lives are not created in a vacuum but are greatly influenced by our interactions with others. The making and re-making of the narratives of our lives involves relations of power. The Project is interested in exploring with community members the ways in which relations of power have influenced the construction of their stories of identity. This sort of exploration is not about imposing the political beliefs of project team members upon community members. It involves instead creating the space for community members to explore their experiences and to locate them within broader relations of power in the culture.

Community members have expressed how helpful it has been to explore the ways in which their experience of hearing voices is strongly located in systems of power and domination within this culture. The troublesome voices they hear are often representative of powerful forces of negativity. Community members have often expressed that they find it liberating to explore the context of the voices and to understand them as voices of dominance. In this way this work is powerfully political. As community members explore the effects of power relations on their lives they often name experiences of gender injustice and experiences of power and domination within the psychiatric system. It is this naming which at times acts as a cornerstone in enabling people to separate themselves from negative ways of understanding themselves and their lives. (project team member)

The Project is interested in locating the experiences of people within broader power relations and exploring the effects of these relations of power. It is also interested in examining the politics or power relations within everyday interactions between project team members and community members. In this way the effects of these power relations can be explored and named, and processes of accountability can be developed so that relationships can be structured in ways that minimise the possibility for abuses of power and maximise the possibilities for creative connections.

We feel it is important that none of the workers deny there is a power relation between us and the community members in the project. Because to deny this means that workers could become engaged inadvertently in practices of domination. When workers acknowledge that the power relation exists it means that we take more responsibility for monitoring its effects on people's lives and dismantling it as much as we are able to. To render it invisible exempts workers from this responsibility. As workers we make it our business to do the best we can to dismantle or deconstruct the power relations in the work. This involves constantly asking questions like: What are some other ways to go about trying to dismantle this power relation? Or: How can we identify the toxic effects of this power relation? (project team member)

Invariably, challenging relations of power leads to a questioning of cultural practices.

(ix) Questioning culture

In order to be a worker in the project I reckon you have to have an interest in questioning the social norms of interaction - the ways in which this culture works. You need to be excited and curious about transcending the taken-for-granted ways of living and thinking in our society. Then it becomes a bit of an adventure - questioning together. (project team member)

The Community Mental Health Project takes the approach that the stories through which we understand and live our lives are profoundly influenced by the dominant stories of our culture. In Western culture there is a dominant belief or 'story' about what it means to be a person of moral worth. This belief system emphasises self-possession, self-containment, self-actualisation, and so on. It stresses individuality at the expense of community, and independence at the expense of connection. These are culturally specific values which are presented as universal, 'healthy', 'human' attributes to be striven for. Many of these ideas of health and well-being are often imposed by mainstream services. The attempt to live up to these dominant ideas of what it means to be a human being can have profoundly negative consequences for people's lives.

The Project questions the validity of these stories. It also questions the cultural practices in everyday interactions and ways of speaking that privilege certain ways of being which are then described as 'normal'. These 'normative' ways of being are generally unobtainable and/or undesirable to community members. Questioning the origin and validity of these practices can be an empowering and invigorating process.

The Project provides an opportunity for project team members and community members to challenge together a lot of taken-for-granted ideas about what it means to be a real person or a whole person in our culture. The project is concerned with not reproducing the venerated notions about what it means to be a person in our culture: to be self-possessed, self-contained and self-actualising. There is a questioning of these concepts and generally an appreciation of how these ideas are part of the subjugation of life rather than anything else. Thinking through these ideas frees workers from any of these goals for other people's lives - goals about getting jobs, or getting out of bed at a certain time of day, or goals about anything at all. It makes it more possible for workers to relate to the purposes that community members have for their own lives that might not have anything to do with reproducing the venerated notions of personhood in our culture. It becomes increasingly difficult to have goals for other people's lives, or to somehow believe that what is good for our lives is good for someone else's. We get to radically question these ideas and this is a really important part of the project's ethos. (project team member)

(x) Acknowledging the political nature of the work

It is a political journey that we are on. These ways of understanding our lives and experiences are so different to the normal, mainstream psychiatric values that we are generally exposed to. It is a political action to be working together like this. It is also a mindful journey. It doesn't just happen by accident. (community member)

The Community Mental Health Project believes that joining with people to name injustice, to question cultural understandings and their effects on people's lives, and to participate in the re-authoring of preferred ways of living, is a political undertaking.

Everyday interactions and circumstances become opportunities to question venerated notions of culture. Project team members need to become very skilled at creating the context for community members to renegotiate some of the ways in which they have understood certain actions and events in their lives. In this way where community members once might have read failure they start to read resistance. They start to see the ways in which their actions have been forms of resistance to what they had been incited to do in their lives. They start to read their actions as resistance to the overwhelming expectations they may have experienced in relation to being a person in this culture. In the process the dominant beliefs and ways of being in our culture are challenged and questioned. (project team member)

In this way, project team members and community members can be seen as companions on a political journey.

In working with project team members they have been advocates but I have also felt that we have been working together in solidarity for this cause, this goal of having a life free from destructive voices. (community member)

(xi) Acknowledging the ways in which the work is mutually enriching

The experiences of both community members and project team members have demonstrated how being 'companions on a political journey' is mutually enriching for all involved. Questioning dominant ways of being in our culture is often accompanied by a sense of invigoration and excitement.

The journey is one of learning and is a two-way process. The giver is the receiver, and the receiver is the giver. We can't be one without the other. It just happens that way. That is sort of the magic of it. We are on a journey together of learning, curiosity and solidarity through the exciting times and the hard times as well. No wonder it is reciprocal. (community member)

I can't meet with the Power To Our Journeys group without feeling inspired. Those meetings finish in the evening and I go away from them really buzzing with thoughts and ideas and reflections on my own life. I can't sleep afterwards! And it's not to do with a sense of being burdened. It's the insomnia of being really excited about possibilities, hopes, about options for action in the face of what seem to be insurmountable difficulties, overwhelming forces. (project team member)

Note

1. First published in the 1997 No.1 issue of the *Dulwich Centre Newsletter*. Republished here with permission.

References

White, M. & Epston, D. 1990: *Narrative Means to Therapeutic Ends*. New York: W.W.Norton.

White, M. 1995: *Re-Authoring Lives: Interviews and Essays*. Adelaide: Dulwich Centre Publications.

2

Saying hullo again:

The incorporation of the lost relationship in the resolution of grief [1]

by

Michael White [2]

Freud ... suggests that the completion of the mourning process requires that those left behind develop a new reality which no longer includes what has been lost. But ... it must be added that full recovery from mourning may restore what has been lost, maintaining it through incorporation into the present. Full recollection and retention may be as vital to recovery and wellbeing as forfeiting memories.
(Myerhoff 1982, p.111)

For some time I have been exploring the 'saying hullo' metaphor and its application to grief work. This exploration has been prompted by particular experiences in therapy with persons who have been diagnosed elsewhere as suffering from 'delayed grief' or 'pathological mourning'. Many of these persons have received intensive and lengthy treatments that have been oriented by the normative model of the grief process, or by the chemical approach to life's problems.

I usually find that such persons are well acquainted with the grief map and can locate their experience in relation to it. They clearly understand that they have failed, in their grief work, to reach the appropriate destination. They 'know' that their arrival at this destination will be evidenced by a fully experienced 'goodbye', acceptance of the permanence of the loss of the loved one, and a desire to get on with a new life that is disconnected from that person.

At first contact, persons experiencing 'delayed grief' or 'pathological mourning' look as if they have lost their own 'selves' as well as the loved one. Without prompting, they put therapists in touch with their loss and its subsequent effect on their life, freely relating the details of their sense of emptiness, worthlessness, and feelings of depression. Such is their despair that I have often felt quite overwhelmed at the outset of therapy. Although I commonly discern invitations from these persons to join in further 'more of the same' conversations that are activated by the 'saying goodbye' metaphor, I am usually able to decline these.

It can be expected that, under these circumstances, persisting with 'grief work' oriented by the normative model will complicate the situation further, rather than empower these persons and enrich their lives. Such is the desolation that these persons experience, establishing a context in therapy for the incorporation of the lost relationship seems far more strongly indicated than further efforts at encouraging the forfeiture of this relationship. My investigation of the 'saying hullo' metaphor was prompted by this consideration.

Guided by this metaphor, I formulated and introduced questions that I hoped would open up the possibility for persons to reclaim their relationship with the lost loved one. Surprised by the effect of these questions in the resolution of the sense of emptiness and feelings of depression, I decided to explore the metaphor further. I expected that a fuller understanding of the processes involved would enable me to more effectively assist persons in the re-positioning of themselves in relation to the death of a loved one, a re-positioning that would bring the relief so strongly desired.

Mary

Mary was forty-three years old when she sought help for what she described as 'unresolved loss'. Some six years earlier, her husband, Ron, had died suddenly from heart failure. This had been entirely unexpected. Until that time, everything had been fine for Mary. She and Ron had enjoyed a 'rich and loving' friendship, one that they both valued very highly.

Upon Ron's death, Mary's world fell apart. Grief-stricken, and feeling 'numbed' from that time, she 'simply went through the motions of life', not experiencing consolation from any quarter. Her numbness survived a number of attempts to 'work through' her grief via counselling. Medication had not provided relief. Despite this, Mary persisted in her attempts to achieve some sense of wellbeing by consulting therapists and 'working on acceptance' over the next five years.

At my first meeting with Mary, she said that she had all but given up hope that she would ever regain even a semblance of wellbeing. She thought she would never be able to say goodbye. After Mary had put me in touch with her despair, I invited her to escape the 'deadly serious' consequences of Ron's death.

I wondered aloud whether saying goodbye was a helpful idea anyway, and about whether it might be a better idea to say hullo to Ron. Further, I said that the desolation she so keenly experienced might mean that she had said goodbye just too well. Mary's response was one of puzzlement and surprise. Had she heard what she thought she had? I repeated my thoughts and saw, for the first time, a spark in her.

I then asked if she would be interested in experimenting with saying hullo to Ron or if she thought he was buried too deep for her to entertain this idea. Mary began to sob; easy sobbing, not desperate. I waited. After ten or fifteen minutes she suddenly said: 'Yes, he's been buried too deep for me'. She smiled and then said that it might be helpful to 'dig him up a bit'. So I began to ask some questions:[3]

- *If you were seeing yourself through Ron's eyes right now, what would you be noticing about yourself that you could appreciate?*

- *What difference would it make to how you feel if you were appreciating this in yourself right now?*

- *What do you know about yourself that you are awakened to when you bring alive the enjoyable things that Ron knew about you?*
- *What difference would it make to you if you kept this realisation, about yourself, alive on a day-to-day basis?*
- *What difference would feeling this way make to the steps that you could take to get back into life?*
- *How could you let others know that you have reclaimed some of the discoveries about yourself that were clearly visible to Ron, and that you personally find attractive?*
- *How would being aware of that which has not been visible to you for the past six years enable you to intervene in your life?*
- *What difference will knowing what you now know about yourself make to your next step?*
- *In taking this next step, what else do you think you might find out about yourself that could be important for you to know?*

Mary struggled with these questions through alternating bursts of sadness and joy. Over the two subsequent sessions she shared with me the important rediscoveries that she was making about herself and life. At follow-up, some twelve months later, Mary said: 'It's strange, but when I discovered that Ron didn't have to die for me, that I didn't have to separate from him, I became less preoccupied with him and life was richer'.

John

John was thirty-nine years old when he consulted me about longstanding 'difficulties with self-esteem'. He couldn't recall not having a critical attitude toward himself. Throughout his life he had hungered for approval and recognition from others. For this, he hated himself all the more, believing that he lacked substance as a person and that this was clearly apparent to others.

John considered himself loved by his wife and children and believed that his experience in this family of procreation had gone some way toward countering his nagging self-doubt - but never far enough. His self-doubt was so easily triggered by what he considered to be the most trivial of circumstances.

He had, on various occasions, sought professional advice, but had not experienced the relief that he was seeking.

In view of the long history of John's self-rejection, I asked for further details about his life. He told me that, as far as he knew, he had a happy childhood until the death of his mother at the tender age of seven, just before his eighth birthday. No-one in the family had coped with this at all well and, for a time, John's father had been a lost person to everyone, including himself. John had vivid recall of the events surrounding his mother's death. He experienced disbelief for some considerable time, always expecting that she would show up around the next corner. He then became entirely heartbroken. Eventually his father re-married to a caring person 'but things were never really the same again'.

I asked John about what difference it would have made to how he felt about himself now if things had remained the same; if his mother hadn't died. At this point he began to get tearful. Didn't he think she might have gone missing from his life for too long? Was it really helpful for her to remain absent from his life? He looked surprised. Would he mind if I asked more questions? 'No, that would be fine.' I proceeded with the following:

- *What did your mother see when she looked at you through her loving eyes?*

- *How did she know these things about you?*

- *What is it about you that told her about this?*

- *What can you now see in yourself that had been lost to you for many years?*

- *What difference would it make to your relationships with others if you carried this knowledge with you in your daily life?*

- *How would this make it easier for you to be your own person, rather than a person for others?*

- *What could you do to introduce others to this new picture of yourself as a person?*

- *How would bringing others into this new picture of your person enable you to nurture yourself more?*

- *In what way would such an experience of nurturing yourself affect your relationship with yourself?*

I met with John on three further occasions at two week intervals, and then for a follow-up eight months later. Over this time, he took various steps to keep his mother's 'picture' of him in circulation, and arrived at a new relationship with himself, one that was self-accepting rather than self-rejecting. He no longer felt vulnerable to those events that used to drive him into self-doubt.

Discussion

Experience of experience

- *If you were seeing yourself through Ron's eyes right now, what would you be noticing about yourself that you could appreciate?*

Those questions that seemed most helpful in assisting persons to reclaim these important relationships, were the ones that invited a recounting of what they perceived to be the deceased person's positive experience of them. This recounting was an expression of their experience of specific aspects of the deceased person's experience. These questions had an immediate and visible effect. The memories that they touched off were not just a factual account of historical events, but a full and vivid re-living of experience, one that incorporated the person's various senses and emotions.

It was clear that, in this recounting, a re-experience of past selves was triggered off. Various lost or forgotten knowledges of self seemed to become available for persons to express. How is this process to be understood?

In striving to make sense of our lives, we face the task of arranging our experiences of events in sequences across time in such a way as to arrive at a coherent account of ourselves. Specific experiences of events of the past and the present, and those that are predicted to occur in the future, are connected to develop this account, which has been referred to as a story or self-narrative.

The past, present, and future are not only constructed but connected in a lineal sequence that is defined by systematic if not causal relations. How we depict any one segment is related to our conception of the whole, which I choose to think of as a story. (Bruner 1986a, p.141)

The success of this task provides us with a sense of continuity and meaning in our lives. We rely on this sense for the ordering of our daily lives and for the interpretation of further experiences. However, this sense is gained at a price. A narrative can never re-present the richness of what Turner (1986) has called our 'lived experience':

> ... *life experience is richer than discourse. Narrative structures organize and give meaning to experience, but there are always feelings and lived experience not fully encompassed by the dominant story.* (Bruner 1986a, p.143)

The structuring of a narrative requires recourse to a selective process in which we prune, from our experience, those events that do not fit with the dominant evolving story that we and others have about us. Thus, over time, much of our stock of lived experience goes unstoried and is never 'told' or expressed.

However, under certain circumstances, it is possible for persons to re-live neglected aspects of their lived experience in un-edited form. At these times the sequential arrangement of events across time is temporarily undone and replaced by what Myerhoff (1982) refers to as 'simultaneity'. Thus, *a sense of oneness with all that has been one's history is achieved* (p.110).

I believe that those questions that invite persons to recount what they perceive to be the deceased person's experience of them, achieve this simultaneity. In this reaching back into experience, alternative and previously lost knowledges can be located and re-performed. Thus, new and enriching acknowledgements and validations of self can become available to persons.

Selection of alternative knowledges

- *What do you know about yourself that you are awakened to when you bring alive the enjoyable things that Ron knew about you?*

In encouraging persons to claim the alternative knowledges that become available in this reliving of experience, I have found other questions to be helpful. These questions invite persons to review this experience and to locate those alternative knowledges of self that present the 'facts' about self that are most appealing; those 'facts' that will assist them and others to 'write' a new story of their lives.

These questions also assist persons in the development of an awareness that:

Every telling is an arbitrary imposition of meaning on the flow of memory, in that we highlight some causes and discount others; that is, every telling is interpretive. (Bruner 1986b, p.7)

Circulation of self-knowledge

- *How could you let others know that you have reclaimed some of the discoveries about yourself that were clearly visible to Ron, and that you find personally attractive?*

As 'self' is a performed self, the survival of alternative knowledges is enhanced if the new ideas and new meanings that they bring forth are put into circulation: *The hard-won meanings should be said, painted, danced, dramatised, put into circulation* (Turner 1986, p.37).

To achieve this circulation, an audience to the performance of such new meanings is required. Questions can be derived that identify and recruit this audience. In the 'reading' of these new meanings, this audience participates, via feedback, in new productions of the person's self. The production of self is a recursive process, one in which selected aspects of one's experience are performed, and in which this very performance contributes to the stock of one's experience of events from which self-knowledge is derived.

Consciousness of production of productions

- *What difference will knowing what you now know about yourself make to your next step?*
- *In taking this next step, what else do you think you might find out about yourself that could be important for you to know?*

Further questions can be introduced that encourage persons to entertain, more fully, their role in the production of their own productions of self. Consciousness of one's production of one's productions opens new possibilities for persons to direct their own course in life.

As persons become aware of the process in which they are both a performer in, and audience to, their own performances, new choices become available to them in regard to the alternative knowledges of self that they might co-operate with - and they experiences themselves as *the authors of themselves* (Myerhoff 1986, p.263).

Other applications

Loss of young child

Parents who have lost very young children have found the 'saying hullo' metaphor helpful, including in the circumstances of the death of unborn children. After being introduced to the idea, they do not experience great difficulty in speculating about what the child's experience of them, as parents, might have been, and then incorporating this.

Child abuse

The applicability of this metaphor has also been explored and found to be helpful with children who have been 'taken into care' with histories of being repeatedly and seriously abused. As a result of such abuse, these children usually relate to their self with hate, and go about doing their best to fail, often mutilating their own lives and futures through destructive behaviour.

In these circumstances, I have worked with the child and residential care workers to locate 'unique outcomes' (White 1988) that identify occurrences of adult persons relating positively and helpfully to the child, instead of negatively and harmfully. These unique outcomes can be located historically and/or currently. For example, it might be discovered that a certain school teacher had taken a particularly kindly attitude towards the child, that a community worker had taken a special interest in the child's plight, or that a residential care worker has recently made some important and pleasing observations about the child.

Once unique outcomes have been established, questions can be introduced that invite the child to render them significant through a performance of meaning. These questions encourage speculation about the alternative knowledges of self that are associated with the unique outcomes. Examples of these questions follow:

- *What do you think it is that your teacher noticed about you that your ... [the abusing adult] was blind to?*
- *What is it about you that told your teacher this?*
- *So what did this teacher know about you that you can know about yourself?*
- *If [the abusing adult] had not been so blind to these facts, and had not missed out on you as a person, what difference would this have made to their attitude towards you?*

These questions, and those that encourage the circulation of the alternative knowledges and a consciousness of the production of one's productions, undermine the child's self-hate and their participation in the mutilation of their own lives and futures.

Adult self-abuse

I have introduced a variation of this work to women and men who, as a result of emotional and/or physical abuse during childhood and adolescence, maintain a very negative and rejecting attitude towards themselves in adult life. This self-rejection is the outcome of their incorporation of the abusing adult/s' attitude towards them.

These persons cannot rest. They feel. perpetually compelled to operate upon and discipline their self according to the abuser's attitudes. They are unable to trust any of the more personally favourable versions of their self that they might encounter through life.

It is helpful to invite these persons to attend to those unique outcomes that identify recent occasions during which they were able to treat themselves with a fraction of 'self-acceptance', or occasions during which they protested their submission to the dominant specifications of self that were established by the abuser.

Once a unique outcome has been identified, questions can be introduced that encourage a specific recounting of childhood and adolescent experiences, one that locates similar but historical episodes of self-acceptance or protest. Efforts are also made to pinpoint the person's age at the time of these historical episodes. Further questions are then helpful in assisting these persons to revise their relationship with their self:

- *If you were looking at yourself through the eyes of that ten-year-old boy right now, what would he be seeing in you that he would really appreciate?*
- *What is it about the development of you as a person that would be most important to him?*
- *Noticing this, would he encourage you to try to be someone else, or would he take you for who you are?*
- *Why do you think he would have liked you for a parent?*
- *What difference do you think it would have made to his life if he'd had you for a parent?*
- *What could you do to side with this ten-year-old boy's attitude towards you, rather than ...* [the abusing adult's] *attitude?*
- *What difference would this make in your relationship with yourself, to how you would treat yourself?*

The responses to these questions contribute to the reclaiming of, and to the performance of, alternative self-knowledges, and to the forging of a new relationship with self through an experience of 'self-specification'.

Separation

The 'saying hullo' metaphor is also appropriate in circumstances where there has been a loss of a relationship that has not been incurred by death. Often, such a loss is devastating to the person who did not initiate the separation and who wanted to persist with the relationship.

One common reaction is for these persons to feel betrayed by their partner, and to submit to extraordinary self-doubt. At times, this is associated with an intoxicating self-righteous anger. These responses usually relate to a new perception that they were never really loved by the other, but 'just strung along'. I refer to this new perception as the 'second story'.

When these responses persist, questions can be introduced that bring the 'first story' - the one that includes the experience of being a lovable person - out from the shadow of the second story; questions that invite the incorporation of the first story, and an active co-operation with it. Successful incorporation resolves the self-doubt and self-righteous anger.

Conclusion

Many persons who have consulted me over problems that relate to unresolved grief have found the 'saying hullo' metaphor, and the questions derived from this metaphor, to be helpful. I have consistently found that, through the incorporation of the lost relationship, those problems defined in terms such as 'pathological mourning' and 'delayed grief' are resolved. In achieving this incorporation, persons arrive at a new relationship with their self. Their attitude towards their self becomes a more accepting and embracing one, and they come to treat themselves with greater kindness and compassion.

The illustrations given in this paper provide some examples of the utilisation of this metaphor. However, these examples by no means exhaust the possible applications.

In focussing here on the 'saying hullo' metaphor, I am not taking a position against the utilisation of the saying goodbye metaphor. There is much to say goodbye to, including to a material reality and to hopes and expectations, etc. Instead, I believe that the process of grief is a 'saying goodbye and then saying hullo' phenomenon.

Having said this, I would argue that every experience of loss is unique, as are the requirements for the resolution of every loss. Any metaphor is only helpful to the extent that it recognises, and facilitates the expression of, this uniqueness, and doesn't subject persons to normative specifications.

Notes

1. First published in the 1998 Spring issue of the *Dulwich Centre Newsletter* (republished here with permission), this paper was prepared for the 'Loss and the Family International Colloquium', Ballymaloe, County Cork, Ireland, 5th-8th July 1988. I would like to thank Karl Tomm for his comments on an earlier draft of this paper.

2. Michael loves living in Adelaide, South Australia, and being with his family and friends. His work with families and communities has attracted widespread international interest. He can also be found swimming, flying a small plane, or riding his bicycle through the Adelaide hills. Michael can be contacted c/- Dulwich Centre, 345 Carrington Street, Adelaide 5000, South Australia.

3. Of course, the examples of questions that are given in this paper are not presented by therapists in barrage-like fashion, but within the context of a co-evolving process. Each question is sensitively attuned to the person's response to the previous question.

References

Bruner, E.M. 1986a: 'Ethnography as narrative.' In Turner, V.W. & Bruner, E.M. (eds), *The Anthropology of Experience.* Chicago: University of Illinois Press.

Bruner, E.M. 1986b: 'Experience and its expressions.' In Turner, V.W. & Bruner, E.M. (eds), *The Anthropology of Experience.* Chicago: University of Illinois Press.

Myerhoff, B. 1982: 'Life history among the elderly: Performance, visibility and remembering.' In Ruby, J. (ed), *A Crack in the Mirror: Reflexive Perspectives in Anthropology.* Philadelphia: University of Pennsylvania Press.

Myerhoff, B. 1986: 'Life not death in Venice: It's second life.' In Turner, V.W. & Bruner, E.M. (eds), *The Anthropology of Experience.* Chicago: University of Illinois Press.

Turner, V. 1986: 'Dewey, Dilthey, and Drama: An essay in the anthropology of experience.' In Turner, V.W. & Bruner, E.M. (eds), *The Anthropology of Experience.* Chicago: University of Illinois Press.

White, M. 1988: 'The process of questioning: A therapy of literary merit?' *Dulwich Centre Newsletter,* Winter, pp.8-14.

PART II

Working
with
Individuals

3

Conversations of ability[1]

by

Alice Morgan[2]

When I was invited to contribute to a newsletter about 'disability' I was very unsure about whether my conversations with Cathryn and her family were suitable. I was unsure if they fitted within notions of 'disability' as their focus has been on ability, competence and the many aspects of Cathryn's life that make her able and strong. Although neurological assessment has confirmed that Cathryn has a mild form of Tourette Syndrome[3], we have shared many stories about aspects of her life that she does not experience as dis-abling.

In this piece, I hope I am able to express the flavour of our meetings and the spirit of our conversations. I will share some of the thinking that has shaped the types of questions I have asked and the directions I have chosen to pursue in our consultations. I will also share some of the dilemmas I have faced as a therapist, working in an area I initially knew so little about.

Background

Bev came to consult me in my role as a school counsellor about Cathryn, her eight-year-old daughter. She was concerned about a number of traits that seemed to be increasing, could happen at any time and with no particular pattern - at least as far as Bev could determine. The trait that most concerned Bev was that Cathryn often opened her mouth very widely in a strained and uncomfortable way before she spoke. Bev told me that Cathryn had some other 'unusual' mannerisms, particularly when speaking in front of others. Bev was concerned that these traits were very different from those of other children and that Cathryn may be teased at school if other children began to notice them. Bev knew that Cathryn had noticed these traits and had started to cry about them.

Whilst remaining attentive to the description of the problem in this initial meeting with Bev, I was also interested in knowing a lot more about Cathryn, as I knew that these traits would not speak totally of her identity. I asked Bev to tell me more about Cathryn - what she liked, what she thought about school, how she liked to spend her time at home and in the holidays, and about her friendships. I heard about Cathryn's love of animals, her interest in making things with wood, her passion for climbing trees, her enjoyment of her visits to Nan and Pa in the country, her love of school, and Bev's knowledge of Cathryn's good ideas.

Spending time to explore these interests and skills was extremely important. Fully appreciating Cathryn as a person, and enquiring about the many aspects of her life, was one of the ways that enabled Bev and I in our conversation to separate Cathryn from the traits that were posing the concern. I assumed that there would be many times separate from the problem of the traits and based my questions on seeking information to support this assumption. This knowledge of Cathryn as a person (not a problem) provided many possibilities for future conversations, began to diminish the influence of the problem in the family's life, and gave me some openings through which to explore possible 'unique outcomes'[4] in future meetings. From time to time I checked with Bev about the direction of the conversation. I was mindful that I didn't want to seem disinterested in her concerns. I didn't want it to seem as if I was brushing her concerns aside or that I wanted to simply 'focus on the positives'. This was not my intention. Bev, however, said that she was interested in the questions I was asking and that she found them helpful. Concern and worry for Cathryn was attempting to disconnect Bev from her knowledge of Cathryn's abilities and competencies. This conversation, according to Bev, helped her 'to remember all the other things that Cathryn does when the habits are not there'.

Bev asked me to meet with Cathryn so that she would 'have someone at school who she can talk to who will understand and try to help'. Bev had arranged an appointment for Cathryn to see a neurologist within a few weeks and said that she would let me know of the outcome of his assessment.

My first conversation with Cathryn

A few days later I met with Cathryn and her pound puppies (toy pets). I spent a lot of our first meeting finding out about Cathryn, her friends, her new house, her cat (Mido), and her dog (Sam). We also talked about playing the piano, violin and recorder, and about how Cathryn likes her present school better than her old one because it has a bigger swimming pool. At some length I also learnt about her pound puppies - where they sleep, what they like doing, when she got them, what they think of living in her pocket, and about the clothes she has so carefully made for them.

Cathryn knew that Bev had talked with me and thought it had something to do with 'what I do with my neck and all the weird things I do'. I immediately re-phrased this statement into externalizing language - hoping to separate Cathryn from the traits. I chose to name the problem 'the habits'. Cathryn thought this was a good name so I asked her, 'what do the habits have you doing?' Cathryn had noticed two habits that made her neck and mouth sore. 'I was wondering what you think of the habits?' I asked, 'Do you like them in your life? How do they suit you?' Cathryn was adamant that she didn't like them and wished she didn't have them.

I asked her about the effect of the habits on:

- *her life*: 'They hurt me. They make my mouth and neck sore.'
- *her relationships*: 'because of the habits mum says 'don't do it' and that's annoying';

- *her friendships*: 'my friends might think I'm stupid';
- *her feelings*: 'I get worried when I'm doing a play because the habits might come on me, mess up the play and other people will think I'm stupid';
- *her school work*: 'the habits do nothing to my school work, they don't get at it';
- *what she thinks about herself as a person*: Cathryn wasn't sure what I meant by this so I asked, 'Do the habits affect what you think about what sort of person you are? Like, do they have you thinking you are a good person or a bad person?' Cathryn said, 'Oh no, they don't say anything about me and what I'm like'.

I was very interested in Cathryn's ability to keep the habits from influencing her school work and her views of herself. I was wondering how she had been able to do this and if this was significant to her too. Before I had the opportunity to ask her about this Cathryn spontaneously offered:

Sometimes the habits don't happen. When I'm concentrating on games or on my work they don't bother me.

'Oh', I replied, surprised that times were already being identified when she was free of the problem's influence, 'Can you tell me some more about what you know about that?'

Well I don't do them (the habits) when I'm not thinking about them.

So ... you've found a way of getting away from them, is that right?

Yeah, when I'm thinking about something else and having fun.

... that gets you away from them?

Yes, but not the crossing-legs habit.

Mmmm.

The crossing-legs habit is hard to get away from - especially on hot days.

So it sounds like you know a bit about some different sorts of habits that try to push you around. Like you've told me about the neck one and the mouth one. What do you know about the crossing-legs one?

I don't like it. It's hard to get to sleep and it makes me hot and sweaty.

So you don't like the crossing-legs one. What do you think about the mouth one and the neck one? Do they suit you and your life?

I wish I didn't have habits happen.

We were nearing the end of our time together on that day so I tried to summarise and clarify what Cathryn had told me. I then asked her if there was anything she wanted to ask me since I'd been asking her lots of questions. She said she wanted to know, 'How do I get these habits and why do I have them?'

I didn't really know how to respond. What do I say? ... I don't know why ... I don't know how ... Honesty seemed a friend. I said that at the moment I wasn't sure about the habits either or what they were up to. But I said that I thought that maybe together we could try to work a few things out about them. I asked her what she thought about that idea - that together we could try to work out a few things about the habits and what they were up to. Cathryn smiled and asked, 'So does that mean I can come another time?' Our future meetings were arranged.

I received a call from Bev a few days later. The neurologist had diagnosed a mild form of Tourette Syndrome. Bev wondered what to tell Cathryn and how best to deal with this new information. She decided it was best to 'play it down' and continue on as normal. Bev worried that prescribing this label to the problem may not assist Cathryn. She told me that Cathryn had enjoyed our meeting and had begun to talk to her about 'the habits'. Bev was interested in this type of conversation continuing.

From this beginning evolved many rich and enjoyable conversations with Cathryn and Bev. Cathryn came on her own sometimes and invited Bev to join us when she was able to. Our sessions often included many of Cathryn's toys who were pretty good at answering questions too! Bev, the toys and a teacher of Cathryn's, Ms Hodge, all became significant people with whom we consulted about the habits from time to time. They were an audience to the new developments and the emerging alternative story.

Further Meetings

Since then I have been regularly meeting with Cathryn, Beverly, the pound puppies, Yowie toys and Tamagochis (electronic pets). As I reflect on the conversations we've shared I can think of about five 'recurring themes' in our meetings. Rather than transcribe every question and response, I'll try to give you some idea of the areas we have talked about.

Before I do so, a slight digression. It may appear by the way in which I am writing that there has been a sequence, a step-by-step nature to our conversations. This is because I am writing as an adult for adults - with a certain order, sequence and structure. This does not accurately reflect how our conversations have occurred. I admire children's ability to discuss many different topics at once. They seem to be able to weave and dart between several topics at the one time, whilst remembering in detail the content of them all. Children, in my experience, are able and prefer to talk in these ways. Gradually I think I am becoming more proficient at keeping up with them. To an adult onlooker the conversations I have shared with Cathryn may appear a bit all over the place and disjointed. And yet I have consistently marvelled at how children retain so much information at one time. A large amount of time was spent with Cathryn talking about her life. Accounts of her daily activities, joys, fun and experiences were inter-woven with the more 'formal' conversations in which 'the habits' were externalized.

The choice of the direction of the conversations was made by Cathryn. I assisted her by keeping track of the different topics that we covered and by consulting her as to what interested her the most to talk about, when we should change direction, and how much or how little she would like to say about particular issues.

I have only included here a few examples of Cathryn's knowledges and responses. There are many more that could have been selected. The following themes or threads recurred throughout our conversations.

Finding out more about the habits

The externalizing conversations continued and the habits were personified and more fully described. I consulted Cathryn in some detail about her experience of the habits and how they worked. We talked about:

- *their tricks and tactics*: We discovered that the habits were quite sneaky and liked to take advantage of certain situations. 'The habits like it when I am bored and don't know what to do. When I'm playing and having fun I don't need to think about them.'

- *what they like and don't like*: 'They really like it when I'm in the classroom, when I'm sitting with the sun on my table. They catch me out - but not always.'

- *how they operate*: 'They don't say things, they just do things to my body.'

- *what warnings they give*: 'With the neck cracking habit I know when it's coming because I get this sliding feeling and I can hear it. It gives me this message and a pulling feeling in my neck. I have to think "go away".'

Cathryn's ability to reduce the influence of the habits in her life

These conversations developed from what Cathryn told me in our first meeting: 'Sometimes the habits don't happen'. As we began to meet regularly, Cathryn was interested in telling me how the previous weeks had been and whether or not the habits had been around. She also talked to me about some of the things that she did to stop the habits sneaking around:

- *having lots to do and keeping busy* (in one session we wrote a list of 27 things that Cathryn was able to do to keep busy and away from the habits);

- *not talking about the habits or giving them attention.*

There were many times when Cathryn told me, in relation to the habits, that she had 'got rid of that one', or, 'that one hasn't been around for ages', or, 'it just hardly ever does that now'.

As I will discuss later, I was often unsure as to how to respond when Cathryn told me these things as I was caught by many dilemmas (see 'My dilemmas' below). I was guided however by curiosity. I continued to ask Cathryn more about what she knew and/or had recently found out. In these discussions I wanted to learn from Cathryn more about what she was able to do to reduce the influence of the habits. I didn't know if, in fact, it was possible to influence them or whether neurological factors would prevent this. I continued to consult Cathryn on her ideas and experience.

One of the habits that Cathryn managed to free her life from was the 'cross-the-leg habit'. I asked her many things about this accomplishment:

How did you do that?

I just open my legs and sort of push them apart.

How long does it take for them to go, when you've pushed your legs apart?

Not very long, they go away then.

How did you come up with that way of dealing with it?

I had to try a few things first and then found that this worked.

What other things did you try?

Sometimes I have a bath or I go the toilet.

How did that go?

That works too sometimes but opening my legs is good.

Bev and Ms Hodge provided a valuable audience to these abilities. I would often consult Bev and Ms Hodge about various things that they had noticed. Bev consistently noticed many things about Cathryn's ability to influence the habits. I asked Bev various questions including:

(i)   How do you think Cathryn did that? Bev replied: *I think she said to herself, 'I don't like it' and told it to 'go away' in her own way.* (I then asked Cathryn if this was how she had done it. She replied that she had tried this and it hadn't worked. This then led to a further clarification of what had worked and what hadn't.)

(ii) What do you think it takes for a person to think about opening their legs to stop the cross-the-leg habit?

Bev replied: *A lot of cleverness and hard work.*

(iii) Is cleverness one of the things you know about Cathryn or is this a new thing that you're just getting to know about?
I've known about her cleverness for a long time. Cathryn is really clever at drawing and playing the piano. (I continued this conversation by tracing the

history of Cathryn's cleverness and asked for some more examples from Bev to more richly describe this quality and ability. I then asked Ms Hodge if she knew about Cathryn's cleverness and she was also able to think of many examples that illustrated a history of cleverness).

Cathryn's ability to train dogs

One of the places that Cathryn most enjoys visiting is her Nan and Pa's farm in the country. Cathryn described to me her joy in climbing the trees, making things from wood in the shed, and her times with Samuel, Daisy and Towser - the dogs. Cathryn spontaneously offered, 'I've trained them to do lots of things'. Cathryn had trained the dogs to sit, to get into cars, to sit on stools, and to complete an obstacle course. She was also teaching them tracking. I was fascinated by this skill. I told Cathryn about my dog and asked her for some ideas about how she went about training.

Cathryn had a wealth of knowledge. She spoke of being firm and clear and how she used different voices to get the dogs to do as she asked them. She told me it can take a few days but if you have all the 'right stuff', all the preparations in place, then you can do it. I asked her a little more about what other people would say about her ability to train dogs and the skills that they have seen she has.

I wondered if this ability to train dogs might be a useful metaphor for training the habits. Did Cathryn think that the skills she has to train the dogs might be handy to use to train the habits? Cathryn really liked the idea of being the boss of the habits, like she could be the boss of the dogs.[5] She told me how she could train the habits - for example, she thought she could 'ignore them' or 'just walk out on them and go and do something else like play on the swings'. I also wondered what was the 'right sort of stuff' that she would need, how long it might take, how she'd be firm, and what sort of voice she would use with the habits. I was very tentative about pursuing these ideas and I wanted to feel confident that the idea appealed to Cathryn. I asked her: 'How much of what you do with the dogs would work on the habits?' Cathryn thought that 'about four or five out of ten' of what she did with the dogs would work on the habits. I then interviewed Bev about what she knew about Cathryn's ability and some of the things that she thought it took to train dogs. Accessing Bev and Cathryn's uncle's voice about Cathryn further enriched the descriptions of Cathryn's skills, knowledges and abilities.

Contribution of the medication to Cathryn's project of taming the habits

About two months after our first meeting, Cathryn was placed on medication to try to alleviate 'the habits'. Since that time the doctor has changed the type of medication and adjusted the dosage in an attempt to determine the most effective treatment.

From time to time the topic of the tablets would come up in our conversations. Bev and Cathryn often had different views about how much the tablet was contributing to the changes they were both noticing.

'If you were to give it a number', I asked Bev one day, 'how much do you think it's been Cathryn's hard work and how much has been the tablet's hard work?'

Oh, 80% Cathryn and 20% the tablet, she replied. Bev would often give Cathryn more credit for her contribution. I asked Cathryn what she thought about the various contributions and she said it was '*about 50/50*'. These opinions then opened possibilities to ask both Cathryn and Bev about their views and to get a richer description of what they both knew.

Recently Cathryn told me: *I think that the habits have almost gone and the tablets make a big difference.* She had also noticed some other changes including *almost forgetting to do things,* and, *I think the tablets are affecting my reading too.* (These changes will be clarified with her doctor.)

Therapeutic letters

From time to time I have written to Cathryn about our conversations. Cathryn tells me that the letters are very special to her and that she keeps them in the drawer in her bedroom. She reads them to remember how she 'can try to stop the habits' and what she can do. Cathryn has taught me to keep these letters short and to resist the temptation to include everything. The following letter was written after four meetings.

Dear Cathryn,

I thought I'd write you this letter about what you told me last Friday. It seems as though you have been working hard on the habits since I spoke to you last and that you have managed to get rid of the mouth habit. WOW! You told me you were able to do this because you got fed up with it and you told the mouth habit it was 'too old' and you 'wanted it to go away'. You also told the habits - 'not now I'm about to have fun'. You said that the mouth habit didn't take too long to get the idea and it was easy to get rid of it. How did you come up with the idea to tell it that it was too old and to go away? How many times did you have to tell it before it got the idea and went away?

Ms Hodge told me that she had also noticed that the mouth habit had gone. Who else would know that you had done this?

I was wondering if you could think of a name for yourself - since you are now able to get rid of the mouth habit? I thought of Cathryn the Habit Buster, or Cathryn the Habit Tamer (like lion tamer). You can probably think of a better name!

You also told me that the habits have come up with a few new tricks lately - like neck-cracking. You said that you don't like the neck-cracking habit because it hurts you and you can't have fun while it's around. Cathryn the Habit Tamer, what do you think you are using to overcome the habits? Cleverness? Having fun? Strength? Courage? Thinking about yourself?

I hope you like this letter and when you read it that it helps you with the habit taming!

Do you want anyone else to know about what you've been able to do?

See you soon, Alice.

My dilemmas

My conversations with Cathryn and Bev have highlighted many dilemmas for me. I have been mindful that conversations are powerfully shaping of people's lives and that this brings with it responsibilities. I wanted to closely monitor the effects of our conversations on Cathryn's life. There were a lot of things that Cathryn told me that reassured me that she was finding our meetings helpful and that they were contributing to reducing the effects of the habits. I tried to attend closely to my dilemmas, however, in an attempt to clarify my thinking, beliefs and practices that were shaping our conversations. Some of these dilemmas are more settled for me now. Practices of accountability have helped. I am pleased, however, that some of the dilemmas remain. They bring an awareness of the need for ongoing vigilance.

Many of my dilemmas centred around using questions of agency. The voice of my dilemmas sounds something like this:

Should I be discussing Cathryn's influence over the habits? If this is a neurological problem then how much influence can she have over them? Is it fair of me to raise these questions when perhaps there is very little chance that she can do anything about them? Am I inflicting an assumption that she can reduce their effects? Do these questions place too much of a sense of responsibility/interest in reducing the habits? Am I setting up false hopes about being able to 'train the habits'?

I hope that the previous discussion of Cathryn's responses to my questions has clarified how some of the dilemmas have become more settled. Cathryn was sure that both her own actions and the tablets were reducing the influence of the habits and were having a positive effect. Always checking with Cathryn about the effects of our conversations seemed crucial. I think that the tone in which I asked my questions was also important - always tentative, unsure, softly spoken, hesitant, wondering and consultative. I would often preface my question with 'I don't know about this but ...'.

I was also unsure about what to do when the habits showed themselves in our sessions. Should I ignore them? What is most helpful? Should I ask Cathryn what to do? What effect would that have on her? I thought a lot about this. At present I give the habits very little attention when Cathryn and I are meeting. I remain interested in focusing on Cathryn - her knowledge, ideas, experience, abilities, life. I think that to focus on the habits may detract from this appreciation. Recently I asked Cathryn what she thought about this dilemma of mine and she said, 'Yeah I think you should ignore them'.

My other major dilemma was that Cathryn had told me that talking about the habits made them worse. She knew the habits liked to be talked about. This worried me. Our conversations did focus on the habits - although they were always externalized. I was concerned that by focusing on them I could contribute to increasing their effects.

I chose to pose this dilemma to Cathryn soon after I discovered that the habits liked to be talked about. I asked her about our conversations and their effects. I told Cathryn that I had been wondering whether she got a hard time from the habits because we talked about them. I asked if she had noticed anything like that. I asked if they came back more when we talked about them. Cathryn reassured me that our conversations were helpful because we 'understood the habits' and that conversations in which people don't know anything about the habits are the ones that make them worse. I think this comment reflects how useful Cathryn and Bev were finding the externalizing conversations. They seemed to be in contrast to many conversations that invited Cathryn to see herself as the problem (rather than separate from it).

My learnings from Cathryn and Bev

The conversations that I have shared with Cathryn, Bev and the toys have contributed significantly to my life. There were so many unknowns in this work. There was very little written about the area that could provide me with clues about how to approach our conversations. I was concerned that I didn't know how to help or what to say. 'Not knowing' is a familiar orientation for narrative therapists, however Cathryn has helped me to feel more comfortable with 'not knowing'. This has meant that I have finely tuned my skills in continually consulting and checking with people about our conversations, trying never to assume that I know what is most interesting and most useful or what is a unique outcome.

I used to think that talking about people's lives, their pets, their interests was an important way of joining with people and building a therapeutic relationship. I was under the misunderstanding that doing too much of this was to go 'off the topic' or somehow to 'digress'. The conversations with Cathryn have helped me to appreciate that spending time talking about people's interests and daily activities contributes in many ways to re-authoring conversations. What I have found particularly interesting is how these parts of people's lives are often separate from a problem's influence.

What stays with me overall though from my conversations with Cathryn is her ability to enjoy, appreciate, savour and make the most of her life. Her joy and involvement in all that she sees and does, her excitement and anticipation for the future, and her delight in new experiences has brought a renewed sense of joy and fun to my life. Perhaps some of her tips about training dogs might also benefit my relationship with Dudley - my Jack Russell terrier.[6]

Notes

1. First published in the 1997 No.4 issue of the *Dulwich Centre Newsletter*. Republished here with permission.

2. When Alice is not walking her dog, Dudley, along the coast of Melbourne, Australia, she enjoys her conversations with people in her private practice and in her role as a school counsellor. She was first introduced to narrative therapy when she studied at Dulwich Centre, and is inspired by continuing to incorporate the ideas in her life. Alice can be contacted c/- Dulwich Centre, 345 Carrington Street, Adelaide 5000, South Australia.

3. Tourette Syndrome is neurologically based and can be accompanied by a wide range of behaviours and mannerisms. See White, M. & Epston, D. 1990: *Narrative Means to Therapeutic Ends*. New York: WW Norton.

4. I was mindful of the possible implications of this choice of language. I wanted to avoid reproducing notions of power, control and/or violence in our conversations and so chose to refer more to training than to 'bossing'.

5. Those interested in knowing more about Alice and the contribution that Dudley plays in her life and work may wish to read her paper in White, C. & Hales, J. (eds), (1997), *The Personal is the Professional: Therapists Reflect on Their Families, Lives & Work*. Adelaide: Dulwich Centre Publications.

4

Her-story in the making:

Therapy with women
who were sexually abused
in childhood[1]

by

Amanda Kamsler[2]

This chapter discusses some of the problematic aspects of the 'traditional' cultural stories about:

- the long-term effects on women of child sexual assault, and

- therapy approaches for working with these women when they identify difficulties in their lives.

Some alternative ideas are outlined about how a therapist can participate with women clients who experienced sexual assault in childhood, to enable them to go beyond the oppression of the dominant, pathologising stories they have about themselves (e.g. stories in which they see themselves as damaged for life), so that they may begin to have access to new, empowering stories about their own resourcefulness and survival. Knowledge gathered from women's stories of their experiences demonstrates how a therapy process that assists clients to locate their experiences in new stories about their resourcefulness leads to them finding and evolving new possibilities for their lives.

Over the last few years I have worked as a therapist in Sydney, Australia, with a number of women who were referred to my practice saying that they were experiencing difficulties which they believed to be related to childhood experiences of sexual assault by male family members or acquaintances. I also work as a consultant for Dympna House, an incest counselling and resource centre for families in which children have been sexually assaulted, and for women who were sexually assaulted in childhood. These experiences have challenged me to re-evaluate my thinking about child sexual assault and to establish clearer ideas about ways of working with the women I see. Ideas outlined in this chapter illustrate some examples from my work and show some applications of these ideas.

For the purposes of this discussion, I propose the following definitions of child sexual assault and incest:

> *Child sexual assault is a sexual act imposed on a young person or child by another person (usually male). The ability to engage a child in a sexual relationship is based on the all-powerful and dominant position of the adult (or older adolescent) offender, which is in sharp contrast to the child's age, dependency, and powerlessness. Authority and power enable the perpetrator to coerce the child into sexual compliance.*
>
> *Incest is any sexual act imposed on a young person or child by another person (again usually a male), taking advantage of his position of power and trust within the family. 'Family' can mean natural parents, step-parents, grandfathers, uncles, brothers, and so on.*[3]

Themes in the literature about the long-term effects on women of child sexual assault

A predominant theme in the literature about the effects of child sexual assault is the notion of psychological damage, which the child undergoes as a result of being sexually assaulted, and which leaves them with long-term impairments and deficits in their personality. Some writers, such as Ellenson (1985), are interested in identifying these women as having a 'syndrome', describing a set of personality variables commonly manifested by women who were sexually abused as children. These writers propose that the behaviour of women may be assessed using certain criteria from traditional psychiatry. These criteria are used to discuss the 'syndrome', so that doctors and others might diagnose the level of disturbance of the women. Blake-White & Kline (1985) have identified the women's symptoms as fitting with the DSMIII category of post-traumatic stress disorder: *Women who experienced incest as a child have the same pattern of symptoms that identify the syndrome* (p.396).

They, and other writers in the field, focus on the 'dissociation process', or the 'repression of emotion' which they observe in women who experienced sexual assault in their childhood. Shapiro (1987) holds the view that the woman's ego is 'shattered' and will require 'rebuilding' after such experiences, and this is another common theme in the literature.

Thus the emphasis of many writers has been on the use of traditional psychiatric classification practices to understand and deal with women's responses to child sexual assault. These ideas have had profound implications for the development of ideas about how therapy should be conducted. The goals of therapy have been described in terms like *helping clients get in touch with repressed emotion; working through feelings; dealing with repressed memories* (Blake-White & Kline 1985, p.398 & 399); and *working through painful experiences and the accompanying guilt and shame, so that conflicts can be revealed, understood, and resolved* (Faria & Belohlavek 1984, p.469). The act of helping clients to understand the meaning of repressed conflicts is said to produce change. The client comes to terms with her repressed feelings, and this leads to changes in behaviour. Overall, the terms used to describe approaches to therapy imply that they are based on ideas about diagnosing the client's pathology, which will then be treated by the therapist.

In applying this framework in therapy, the context for the development of the woman's problems is not considered. The attention of therapists has been focussed on ideas like the 'seductive child', or 'pathological mother'. A significant effect of this individual pathology focus is that therapists may overlook the contribution of the perpetrator's interactions with the woman to the development of her perceptions about herself and the world. This effect is understandable in view of the way that the psychiatric literature about incest has largely referred to psychodynamic theory. In the literature,, blame has been shifted away from the perpetrators and onto the victims. Waldby (1987) and Ward (1984) provide a clear discussion of the historical origins of this shifting of blame. Elizabeth Ward refers to the clinical literature on incest and finds 'stunning testimony' to what feminist theorists Stanley & Daly have named 'agent deletion'. She describes how the language used in the literature *subliminally establishes the wives and daughters as the active parties and the fathers as passive puppets* (p.134). Her extensive discussion contains graphic examples from the clinical literature which are *couched within a cobweb of the same old blame-the-victim mythology* (p.157).

The literature from family psychiatry offers another set of themes about ways of considering the long-term effects on women of child sexual abuse. This body of theory proposes that family dysfunction is the explanation for the existence of incest. The family as a unit is seen as pathological, and symptoms signify overall current family maladjustment. The dysfunctional incestuous family is one in which 'normal' family hierarchies based on age and sex have broken down. This breakdown is attributed almost completely to mothers who are frequently seen as failing to fulfil their nurturing and protective roles toward the children and their wifely role to the father (Lustig et al. 1966; Justice & Justice 1979).

Pathological relationships are viewed as the therapeutic issue, and the occurrence of incest is perceived as a symptom of this. Incest is seen as serving the function of holding together a family system whose internal relationships are unstable: *We propose that incest is a transaction which serves to protect and maintain the family in which it occurs* (Lustig et al. 1966, p.39).

Furniss (1983) supports the idea that incest is a symptom of family dysfunction, saying that: *the development of the incest dyad between father and daughter is strongly influenced by problems in the mother-daughter and mother-father dyad* (p.267).

His discussion of the father-daughter dyad focusses mainly on the daughter's contribution, and his discussion of the mother-daughter dyad focusses mainly on the mother. It is notable that the perpetrator's contribution is only briefly mentioned (Calvert 1984). McCarthy & Byrne (1988) recently made the following statement when commenting on their hypothesis about the link between 'ambivalent social relations' and the generation of incest:

> *... it seems as if the increased occurrence and disclosure of father-daughter incest is a 'socially situated' phenomenon reflecting the confusion at the heart of the modern family. It is an apparent paradox that this phenomenon is a particular family's somatic expression of its struggle to be child-centred, to shift its gender roles, and to value emotionality, proximity, and non-hierarchical social relations.* (p.183)

Once again, the significance of the father's behaviour is obscured in this statement.

Concepts from family therapy such as the view that incest serves a function for the family, or that it may be a family defence against loss (Gutheil & Avery 1977), suggest particular directions for therapy of adult women who experienced child sexual abuse. Therapists operating from these points of view will focus on assisting women to become more 'functional' according to certain criteria for 'normal' family relationships. For example, Deighton & McPeek (1985) describe a family of origin treatment approach in which women in a group are coached to develop a more objective stance with family members and to resolve interpersonal issues with them. They write about the benefit of this being that women begin to see *that the adult perpetrator and the non-involved parent were victims too* (p.408). The authors emphasise the *responsibility of the woman in changing her position relative to family of origin members* (p.410).

These ideas about family dysfunction all obscure the operation of power relationships implicit in incest, and serve to protect the perpetrator and de-emphasise his responsibility. Waldby (1987) says that: *the daughter's experience is effectively denied by this therapeutic focus, which regards the actual incestuous relationship as a red herring, whose pursuit may actually impede treatment* (p.15).

In emphasising the idea that family dynamics should be the focus for therapy, rather than the incest itself (e.g. Machotka 1967), many authors suggest that therapists working with families where incest has occurred assign responsibility to all family members as if they are equally culpable. They see any strong focus on the role of fathers as inappropriate. Thus, therapy based on these notions involves members having to adjust their behaviour to more appropriate roles - particularly, it seems, the traditional roles of mother and daughter.

Thus, while these therapeutic approaches acknowledge the importance of the family context for the development of the woman's problems, they do so in a way which, once again, obscures the power relationship the perpetrator had in his interactions with her in childhood. I believe that these frameworks for therapy promote blindness (or, at best, insufficient attention) on the part of the therapist to the responsibility of the perpetrator in shaping the woman's responses and future. As with frameworks which rest on ideas of pathology and diagnosis, the significance of the broader social context is ignored or glossed over in descriptions about these approaches to therapy.

An alternative view

I agree with Herman (1985) that it is *an exaggeration to claim that* [child sexual assault and] *incest inevitably leads to lasting emotional distress* (p.88). It is important to note that, as Herman comments, data on long-term effects of father-daughter incest are derived entirely from clinical reports, i.e. studies of women who identified themselves as patients in need of mental health services. She refers to Tsai's (1979) survey which indicated that at least some women with a history of child sexual assault perceive themselves as relatively well-adjusted in adult life, and that this correlated well with clinical assessments. These women acknowledged the trauma of child sexual assault, but believed they had escaped long-term distress by receiving helpful intervention from other people, such as family members and teachers.

I hold the view that child sexual assault does not necessarily lead to long-lasting 'intrapsychic damage', e.g. 'shattered ego'. The way I understand what has happened to the women I see in therapy is that they suffer difficulties in their adult life in response to repeating oppressive patterns of interaction in their family and other significant contexts. My perspective is interactional and contextual, rather than intrapsychic and psychodynamic.

The more traditional intrapsychic perspectives view the client as having some kind of pathology which the therapist, as an expert on pathology, will fix through 'diagnosis' and 'treatment'. The implication of this way of thinking is that somehow the damaged personality of the client will be understood and repaired through the expertise of the therapist's interventions. (For further discussion about the implications of various ways of seeing the therapy process, including this way, see Epston & White 1989).

In contrast to this, a contextual, interactional perspective does not see the development of difficulties as taking place inside the person and as being pervasive to their personality. Instead, attention is paid to the various interactional contexts within which a person's difficulties may emerge.

A contextual way of viewing how difficulties may develop in the life of a woman who was sexually abused in childhood

- The experience of being sexually abused will initially lead to the young child having an array of confusing and overwhelming feelings, which strongly affect her perception of herself, e.g. she may begin to see herself as bad and dirty and believe she is to blame for the abuse. This is often encouraged by the perpetrator of the abuse, who may work very hard to ensure that the secret about the abuse is kept.

  Based on these experiences, the feelings and beliefs she begins to develop about them, the child begins to develop ways of dealing with her life, e.g. secrecy, and blaming herself when things go wrong, which serve to reinforce her feelings and beliefs about herself.

- Following the child's experience of abuse and the establishment of patterns of behaviour and thinking like secrecy and self-blame, the child responds to family members and others in ways which lead them to consider her 'naughty' or 'disturbed', e.g. she may act out sexually, be aggressive, or have mood swings. They will respond to her in the ways they usually do when they perceive her as being naughty or disturbed - e.g. punishment, or seeking professional help. The perpetrator of the abuse may also be continuing the abuse. All of these interactions serve to reinforce (a) the patterns of behaviour around secrecy, and (b) the beliefs the child is developing about herself - e.g. 'I'm no good'. The family context may become a life-support system for these interactions and beliefs, which continue to have a negative effect on her view of herself and on her experience of relationships.

- Disclosure about the abuse may exacerbate the beliefs and behaviour, if the child is not believed. Alternatively, if the child is believed and supported, there may be a significant interruption of the kinds of interactions which secrecy encourages, e.g. more openness may be possible between the child and her mother and siblings. New interactional patterns, challenging secrecy, and self-blame, and the breaking of more family silences, become possible.

- If disclosure does not occur, or if the child is not believed and she continues to be influenced by secrecy and self-blame, her experiences as an adult woman of interactions in other significant relationships may further promote the survival of habitual responses and beliefs, e.g. she may blame herself or see herself as damaged if there are sexual problems in her relationship with her partner. She may seek professional help for herself and receive a diagnosis which serves to confirm her view of herself as a damaged person.

Details about the implications of this perspective for therapy will be discussed later in this chapter.

These ideas about the process of the development of difficulties for women who have been sexually assaulted as children are similar to those described by Durrant (1987). He talks about the experience of sexual abuse as one in which the child will have had no control over events when the abuse occurred. This experience of 'out-of-controlness' may be exacerbated by events that follow the abuse, e.g. the disbelief of other people. Durrant describes how the child may become caught up in a cycle of out-of-control behaviour and emotion, and how the distress may affect all aspects of her experience of herself. This process may continue into adult life.

I believe it is important to include, in this description about the child's family context, an acknowledgement of who it was that had control, i.e. who had the power to define the child's experience, and how was this achieved? I am interested in the notion of including acknowledgement of the responsibility of the perpetrator of the abuse in an account of the development of the woman's difficulties and beliefs about herself. Clearly, there are often other significant relationships which play an important part in shaping a woman's view of herself. I am paying particular attention here to the woman's experience of the relationship with the man who abused her, as I believe this has been neglected in the literature.

Oppressive stories authored by perpetrators of child sexual abuse which influence the stories women who were abused tell about themselves[4]

These ideas are drawn from conversations with women about their experiences in their relationships with men who sexually abused them.

- It is usually the case that the perpetrator of the abuse has overtly or covertly conveyed to the victim the message that she was to blame for being abused, e.g. 'you led me on', 'you shouldn't dress like that - you were asking for it', 'this is all you are good for'. The perpetrator generally denies responsibility for the abuse, for its impact on the child's life and for the consequences to the family. This idea is strongly reinforced for the victim by messages she receives from the surrounding social context, e.g. 'only bad girls get raped', 'children are seductive', 'women who get raped must have asked for trouble', and so on. These interactions with the perpetrator will establish the conditions for the development and survival of habits such as self-blame and self-hate. These ways of thinking may permeate the woman's stories about herself.

- The perpetrator will often actively promote secrecy by enforcing it with the child or young woman so that she is divided from other family members. As a child, the woman often had no opportunity to check out her own reality because of the rule of secrecy. This contributes to her sense of isolation and confusion, which are devastating side-effects of secrecy. The perpetrator has the power to create a reality for the abuse, perhaps saying things like, 'all fathers do this', or, 'this is for your own good', or, 'you really like this', or, 'this is our special secret', to justify his actions. All of this may contribute to the development of self-doubt in the woman's life, as the perpetrator's account of events has had precedence over her own. She may also become vulnerable to erasing her own feelings in response to this.

- The child's interactions with the perpetrator may have encouraged in her feelings of enormous responsibility for others. He may have directly suggested to her things like, 'I'll be sent away if you tell', or, 'your mother will have a breakdown if you tell her', or, 'you're the only one who understands me', or, 'I'll go and do this to your little sister if you refuse'. These kinds of ideas might be less directly implied. The effect of this is that the woman has received intensive instruction in putting others' needs first and her own last, and this may become an habitual pattern in her story about relationships.

- The various ways in which the perpetrator exerted control over the child - either subtly or directly, e.g. intimidation, violence - in order to continue to have access to her to meet his needs, may promote the development of habitual responses of fear and panic in intimate relationships when she becomes an adult. Fears may figure prominently in stories she tells about herself (Laing & Kamsler 1988).

Therefore, the woman who was sexually abused in childhood may be seen as not simply under the influence of the past, as Durrant (1987) suggests, but also under the influence of a number of prescriptions for how to feel, be, and think, which were actively promoted by the perpetrator in his interactions with her.

It is clear that there is a high degree of fit between many of these prescriptions and the predominant role definitions for women which are expressed in patriarchal ideology. Indeed, Waldby (1987) comments:

The kernel of the feminist understanding of incest is formed by the assertion that father-daughter sexual abuse is a particularly intense variant of 'normal' male-female relations in a patriarchal society. (p.17)

She quotes O'Donnell & Craney's (1982) idea that the incest victim *bears the quintessence of female oppression* - she is introduced to *the role of the powerless, dutiful, submissive wife* (as mentioned in Waldby 1987, pp.17 & 19). The child's interactions with the perpetrator can be described as 'intensive training' for her in fitting with the stereotypical submissive female role. The groundwork has been thoroughly prepared for the woman to respond in strongly gendered ways in other significant relationships. She may begin habitually to apply the perpetrator's prescriptions to herself in numerous situations, e.g. putting her own needs aside and developing a 'being for others' lifestyle in her relationships, being passive, being obedient. Thus, the effect of these interactions in childhood may be that she conforms even more strongly to gender prescriptions for women. This perspective about women experiencing the disempowering effects of a relationship which echoes the oppressive arrangements between men and women in society is missing in most of the writings about therapy in the area of child sexual assault.

To sum up, I believe that the significance of the whole context of a woman's experience has been insufficiently explored in the literature which discusses ways of doing therapy with women who were sexually assaulted in childhood. The woman's life is viewed entirely through an intrapsychic lens in the majority of articles about the long-term effects of child sexual assault. A consideration of the significance of her experience of interactions with the perpetrator in the development of problems, together with the influence of ideas from the broader social context, is entirely left out in many articles and books. This omission frequently leads the therapist to consider the difficulties presented by the woman in therapy as being related to her individual pathology or to dysfunctional family relationships. I believe it is crucial for a therapist to operate from a framework which allows issues from both the woman's familial and social context to be accessed and addressed in therapy.

Framework for Therapy

Theory about development of problems

The framework for therapy that I have started from in working with women is the approach being developed by Michael White, which was initially based on Bateson's cybernetic notions of restraints and information. The pivotal ideas about restraints in cybernetic theory suggest some useful ways to consider the situation of women who were sexually abused as children. The approach understands the development and consolidation of problems in terms of the idea that events take their course because they are restrained from taking alternative courses (White 1986, p.169).

A therapist operating from this perspective constructs the situation of people presenting problems as being a consequence of the operation of retraining beliefs and assumptions about themselves and their world. These beliefs and assumptions do not allow them to have access to alternative solutions to their difficulties. This is because information which does not fit with the restraints is screened out and not perceived. This way of constructing things allows the therapist to view the development of problems as occurring in the context of habitual thoughts and feelings and repeating interactional patterns which prevent the person from having certain information about their own resources which may be useful in solving the problems they are struggling with. For example, a woman who was sexually abused in childhood may habitually blame herself for the abuse and be unable to 'notice' the perpetrator's contributions to the situation. She can be described as being blind to other information which might assist her in responding differently to the past and present relationships. Clients are seen as being out of contact with information about their own resources which might assist them in handling problems as a result of the operation of restraints. This concept allows us to understand how it is that clients repeatedly apply the same attempted solutions despite the fact that they may in fact perpetuate the problem.

I have already described examples of restraining ideas and patterns in my discussion about the impact of the woman's childhood interactions with the perpetrator, e.g. secrecy.

Here is an example of the way restraints contribute to a woman habitually applying solutions which perpetuate the problem:

A child is sexually abused by her father who tells her, 'All fathers do this - what are you getting upset about?' However, she is upset and anxious and eventually tells a teacher who does not believe her and tells her not to worry about it. She decides not to tell anyone else. The child believes it is she who has the problem and blames herself for the abuse, and this idea restrains her from making a different response. As an adult, whenever she thinks about what happened to her, she doesn't tell anyone and continues to think it was her fault. Secrecy and self-blame become strong influences in her life and relationships. Her distress increases - the more this happens, the more she blames herself, and it becomes even harder to think about telling someone.

Recently I have employed White's idea of a text analogy for therapy (White & Epston 1989) which gives another description of the approach. Using this analogy, the development of problems is seen as taking place in the language and conversation of those most concerned about them. People who present to therapists with problems are seen as being intensely focussed on 'problem-saturated' descriptions about their situation, and as being out of touch with their capacity to be successful in the face of their difficulties. Problems are seen as a story or idea with a history and a future - as being directional, as having a lifestyle support system, and as being progressive, i.e. they are located in a sequence of events across time. People presenting for therapy are said to have co-evolved with others significant to them around certain realities, and the 'dominant story' they tell about themselves (i.e. the problem-saturated description) has been reinforced in many ways, leaving no space for them to perform another story - the story about unique outcomes, or occasions where the person was in fact able to have some impact over the problem. Events are interpreted through the lens of this dominant story, which shapes the way persons attribute meaning to their experiences.

Here is an example of how the person's 'dominant story' restrains them from having access to their own resources:

A woman called Alice was referred to me - she was having persistent nightmares, was very concerned that she found it hard to sustain relationships with men, and saw herself as being irrational and disturbed. She said she had been sexually abused over six years by her grandfather when she was a child, and had been physically and emotionally abused by her mother, father, and stepmother. She believed that she was a 'mess' and, although she thought this was to do with her past experiences, she had accepted family members' views of her as being emotionally disturbed. In her own words, 'I'm fucked'. She seemed to have the view that she was a damaged person who was possibly beyond repair. This story pervaded her descriptions of herself so strongly that she was initially unable to identify any information about herself which deviated from the view that she was a 'mess'. She persistently blamed herself for her situation and put herself down - in her own words, 'I had a total belief that I was a difficult and unlovable person'. This story was reinforced in her interactions with all family members who responded to her distress by rejection or withdrawal, and this seemed to lead to her experiencing increased distress which would lead to them seeing her as more disturbed, and so on. This story was also perpetuated in her experience of interactions in other significant relationships throughout her life.

I will refer to Alice's story in more detail later in this chapter.

In addition to the concepts I have described, I am interested in the idea that the stories people have developed about themselves are located in the context of certain ideologies which are cultural and socio-political stories. White has drawn on the work of Foucault in elaborating this idea, and suggests that therapy can be a context for challenging the way the ideologies, or dominant knowledges, operate. In relation to incest, I believe the dominant knowledges which influence women in constructing their personal stories are patriarchal ideology and the whole area of psychiatric diagnosis and classification. These are the linguistic and epistemological contexts in which incest has traditionally been located.

Therapy

What follows from these ideas about problem-development is that a context for change can be established through the therapist working to promote double description extensively in therapy. This means that the therapist works with clients to develop many new descriptions of events in order to generate 'news of difference which makes a difference' (White 1986), i.e. to challenge or loosen restraints, including the restraining beliefs from patriarchy and psychiatry. Clients need to be able to draw distinctions, to perceive a contrast between their own description and a new description, for them to receive news of difference or new information. This process triggers new responses which make it possible for them to see new solutions. The new description is co-evolved with the therapist participating actively in introducing new descriptions, often in the form of questions, and building on these new descriptions in response to the client's responses.

As Munro (1989) says:

Double description challenges restraints, thus triggering new solutions. For example, the second description and the new perceptions this offers, enables clients to experience a view of the problem [and of themselves] *which is not bound by the restraints under which their first description operated.* (p.185)

The therapist assists the client to develop the new description in a variety of ways which White elaborates in his articles and teaching, e.g. externalizing problems, relative influence questions, collapsing time, raising dilemmas, and responding to responses (White 1986).

These foundation ideas about the approach have been extended in a new direction recently in White's re-description of his work, which he believes fits best with a text analogy for therapy. Clients are seen as being under the influence of a dominant story about themselves, their relationships, and the problem itself. Their descriptions of themselves are understood to be dictated by the dominant story, and the many alternative stories which they could potentially express about their competence and resourcefulness are not given space to be performed. It seems to me that restraints are the beliefs and patterns of interaction that support the dominant story.

The goal of therapy is. to invite clients to access aspects of their experience of themselves which have been edited out of the dominant story. The critical steps in assisting clients to locate alternative stories about themselves will be described, together with examples from my work with women who were sexually assaulted in childhood.

Externalizing the problem

Tomm (1989) has described the therapeutic activity of externalizing the problem, which is central to the practice of this approach, as *a linguistic separation of the distinction of the problem from the personal identity of the* [person]. He believes that this process *opens 'conceptual space' for* [people] *to take more effective initiatives to escape the influence of the problem in their lives* (p.54). The effect of externalizing the problem is to begin to undo some of the negative effects of diagnosis and labelling. I believe this is of profound importance in the area of child sexual abuse where, as I have described, there has been a tradition of applying pathologising, static labels to women. The labelling process encourages conversation in terms of diagnosis. This supports the view that the problem is the woman herself, and reinforces self-blame and guilt. Externalizing the problem is the first step in inviting the woman to separate herself from the effects of labelling, and this leads to the possibility of her noticing alternative stories about herself as a person who at some times has not let the problem entirely overtake her life.

As White (1988/89) says:

> *From this new perspective, persons* [are] *able to locate 'facts' about their lives and relationships that could not even be dimly perceived in the problem-saturated account ... facts that provided the nuclei for the generation of new stories.*

The conversations I had in therapy with a woman called Beth contained some examples of externalizing the problem. Beth told me in our early meetings about how she had disclosed to family members that her father had sexually abused her over a number of years when she was a child. She talked extensively about her guilt over the abuse and her fears about coping with life. These feelings had at times in the past pushed her into attempting suicide and believing she was having a 'breakdown'. I externalized secrecy initially, and invited Beth to map its influence on her life and relationships. Fear, guilt and super-responsibility for others appeared to be the major effects, and I externalized each of these, e.g. asking her about what impact fear had had in her life and on her relationships.

Locating the dominant story in the context of interactions, and in the wider social context

Once the problem has been externalized, the dominant pathologising story which the woman tells about herself is externalized. I believe it is helpful to assist her to locate where this story came from and to develop some ideas about how it became so influential over time. Questions can be introduced, such as: 'How was secrecy encouraged by other people in your life?', 'How was secrecy enforced?', 'What training did you get at favouring others over yourself?' These kinds of questions allow the woman to begin to gain access to the contributions of others, through their interactions with her, to the development of the difficulties she faces. I believe that eliciting a full picture of this is very important, as it facilitates the naming of the oppressive practices which have allowed the effects of child sexual assault to survive. This further assists the woman to separate from the pathologising picture she has of herself, because she becomes more aware of the whole context of her own experiences, including the context of her interaction with the man who abused her, e.g. when I asked Beth what training she thought she had received in super-responsibility, she talked with me about the ways in which her father had intimidated her so that she would comply with his demands on her (sexual and otherwise); her life as a child became focussed on ensuring that she looked after his needs as a priority.

Questions may potentially be introduced which can assist women to locate their experience of the problem in terms of the limiting effects on them of bigger, socio-political stories or ideologies. For example, I asked Beth whether she thought that there are ideas in society which might support habits of super-responsibility for women. She readily identified many examples, and together we explored the consequences of this for her as a person. White's (1986) paper on anorexia suggests some useful directions for questions which give women an opportunity to assess the impact on them personally of society's prescriptions for women.

Relative influence questions

This approach contains some very helpful ideas about how to invite clients to re-tell their story in such a way that they have access to their experience of their own resourcefulness in the face of the problem (White 1988, 1988/89). Two categories of questions can be introduced - one to map out the details and effects of the dominant story, e.g. 'What influence have fears had on your life? on your relationships with other people?', and one to begin to map out the 'unique outcomes', or the occasions where the woman experienced some influence in her own life despite the power of the dominant story. For example, any disclosure of sexual abuse is a direct attack on secrecy, and is a unique outcome. A woman may be asked whether she had ever told anyone she was sexually abused, and this could be followed by an exploration, e.g. 'How was it that you defied the secrecy when you disclosed about your father abusing you?' It is crucial that a thorough exploration of the first category of questions, about the dominant story, is entered into before unique outcome questions are introduced.

It is not my intention to cover the many and varied ways a client can be invited to identify unique outcomes. However, when the therapist asks unique outcome questions like, 'Was there an occasion when you could have been stopped in your tracks by fear but you withstood it instead?', space is opened for the client to begin to author an alternative story about herself.

Questions to invite an elaboration of the alternative story

The client is invited to 'perform meaning' around the unique outcomes which are identified. The kinds of questions asked ensure that the woman is able to attribute personal meanings to events, and to experience the impact of the new emerging story. This is a prerequisite for the survival of the new story. The client is invited to locate a full account of the unique outcomes in a new, alternative story about her lived experience. The goal of this is to ensure that the person experiences the full significance of the unique outcomes. This process of inviting people to go back to their own experience and bring forth alternative stories about themselves leads to them having a different experience of themselves. The role of the therapist throughout therapy could best be described as co-author of these emerging alternative stories.

The following questions came from my conversations with Beth:

- *How was it that you defied secrecy and your father's training in putting others first when you disclosed about the abuse?*

When Beth identified some other occasions when she had put herself first, I enquired about them in detail:

- *How were you able to do this?*

- *How did you give yourself priority?*

- *How do you account for the fact that you felt strong enough to withstand the habit of putting others first?*

- *How did you withstand your father's training?*

- *What did you experience?*

- *What difference has this made to your experience of yourself?*

- *What does this tell you about yourself that you didn't realise before?*

- *How could you bring your friends up-to-date with this development?*

There are countless ways a therapist can participate with the client to develop and extend the alternative story. White's papers outline the kinds of questions which appear most likely to further the co-authoring of alternative stories.

The application in therapy of ideas such as externalizing problems and unique outcome questions allows the therapist to assist the woman to locate her experience in the context of family interactions, including the relationship with the perpetrator. It also allows her to locate her experience in terms of the broader socio-political context. In the process of therapy, the woman has the opportunity, in conversation with the therapist, to discover information about herself and her resources. This leads to her responding in ways which pave the way for change. The emphasis here is on the idea of the client as expert, with the therapist's role being to ask questions which generate unique outcomes and new stories. This is in contrast to more traditional ways of doing therapy where the therapist is seen as the expert who has the knowledge to diagnose and fix the client's problems.

The approach outlined here taps knowledges a woman has about herself and her strengths, which have been buried as a result of the operation of the dominant story. When the woman is invited to separate herself from the dominant story, and new information is generated, the dominant knowledges which the woman drawn upon to define herself are thereby challenged, and new responses and solutions become available to her.

The Story of Alice:
An illustration of the therapy process[5]

Alice is a woman I have seen in therapy over the last two years. She has agreed to allow me to share this story, which includes her comments on her experience as a client, which she decided to write down as a way of reviewing it for herself.

Alice was referred to me by a therapist at Dympna House, where she had participated in a self-help group for incest survivors. When she contacted me to make an appointment, she said she wanted help in two areas:

- Handling her nightmares. Over the last two years she had been experiencing long periods of disturbed sleep as a result of terrifying dreams. The nightmares would persist over months, occasionally disappear for short periods, then suddenly recur for months on end.

- When she was involved in relationships with men she would feel comfortable for a short time, but end up feeling revulsed in sexual situations. She would often finish relationships based on this. She saw this as being related to her experiences of sexual abuse.

Alice said that she had sought therapy earlier in her life to deal with her distress about her family and with her memories about being sexually abused by her grandfather. Individual and group therapy had helped to some degree, and she said that she had felt that she was not so alone on learning that the experience of child sexual abuse was a common one among women. However, despite her previous attempts to get help, she was still feeling very distressed and confused about her life.

Sessions 1-3

Alice began by presenting to me her concerns about her nightmares and relationships. She also talked about her experiences of being sexually abused by her grandfather from age four to age eleven. Her parents had separated in the UK when she was three years old, and her father was given custody of her as her mother was seen as being 'emotionally unstable'. She and her father came to Australia, where her father met and married his second wife. It was this woman's father who sexually abused her. She described how she had disclosed about the sexual abuse to her stepmother during adolescence, but was not believed until her stepsister disclosed that the same thing was happening to her. No action was ever taken outside the family over this - the stepmother confronted her father, but did not support Alice. Alice described the ongoing conflict which she had with her stepmother and father, which led to her being asked to leave home at seventeen. In Alice's view, every interaction with members of her family - including the infrequent contact with her mother - was an experience of rejection and invalidation.

The focus of the first three sessions was not on nightmares, sexual abuse, or current relationships with men. Alice talked with me in detail about her worry about therapy and her distrust of therapists. I took the sessions slowly, believing that her worry about trusting me was an important restraint in the relationship with me. I asked her to simply consider the risks of getting involved in therapy and to begin to keep track of the occurrence of the nightmares in a diary.

Alice noticed during the first three sessions that she was experiencing more sadness, and began to talk about how difficult and uncomfortable it was for her to show her feelings to other people. This she saw as a big risk in being involved in therapy where she might get more in touch with herself and her needs and feelings. She voiced her fear that 'there is so much there' that she wasn't sure that she or the therapist would cope. I externalized her habit of hiding feelings, and we explored the effect of this on her life. I discovered that she had received training from family members in not showing feelings as this meant she was 'irrational' and 'bad' like her mother was. Her mother was portrayed to her as incompetent and volatile. She said that she had learnt by her experiences of rejection and the disbelief of other family members when she was upset that no-one could handle her feelings, so she just coped on her own with them. We talked about how she had learnt not to be herself, developing the habit of being someone else's kind of person rather than being her own person (another externalization) in response to family members' requests to not be so emotional. She talked about her isolation, and cried about how sad she felt that no-one in her family had supported her or believed her distress about the sexual abuse.

I began to attempt to get a picture of the unique outcomes by asking Alice whether there had ever been occasions where she had rebelled against these habits and prescriptions and been herself in relationships. She identified occasions where she had taken risks and asked for support from friends. I asked her to supply some details about how she had been able to do this, given the intensive training she had had in not being herself and hiding herself. I also talked with her about how it was she was able to challenge the training, in allowing herself to feel so much during our meetings.

During the first three sessions, Alice's nightmares disappeared - the more she acknowledged her sadness and fear, the less she experienced it at night. She also took the step of contacting the state welfare department and giving them information about her grandfather, although she did not lay charges. I responded to this information with questions to extend the account about unique outcomes, e.g. how had she had the courage to be herself in these situations? It was in session 3 that Alice first talked with me about her habits of peeling skin off her face and arms, and of bingeing and vomiting. She had never told anyone about these habits before. I externalized them, using the word 'habits' to describe them. I believe this was another breakthrough in Alice challenging the effects of her training in not being herself. Alice said quite strongly that she did not wish to focus on these habits as they were not really that much of a problem at present. This continued until later in therapy.

Sessions 4-6

Alice continued to report having nightmare-free nights and to make changes in being more open about her vulnerability to friends and some family members. She made further disclosures to me about being violently physically abused by both her mother and stepmother, and we talked about how this had fed her developing habit of not being herself, of self-invalidation and self-depreciation (further externalizations). It became clear to me from her descriptions about feeling ripped off by others in her family that the sexual abuse was only one way in which Alice had experienced invalidation of herself as a person.

An important focus of this part of the therapy was on seizing on any information Alice gave me about unique outcomes, e.g. times she was open to other people about her feelings. I would elicit the details around these events to allow for a performance of meaning about her escape from her habits of self-invalidation. I was also able to develop with Alice an account of her survival strategies when she was growing up, so that I might understand how she had stopped herself from being completely overtaken by self-invalidation. She recounted her story of survival as a child by describing how she wrote stories and poetry which expressed her feelings. This was a special and precious thing she did when she locked herself in her room, to have breathing space from family conflicts. I asked her whether there were any survival strategies which she had continued to use in the present, and she identified that she was still valuing her own self-expression through singing and occasionally through writing songs. She was able to tell me that she was removing herself from some situations where she was feeling 'done over'. I described this as trusting herself, and as going against her habit of self-invalidation. Once again, I explored the details of these occasions of self-validation to encourage a performance of meaning around them.

Alice made further small but significant changes in the direction of valuing herself and being more true to herself. However, she frequently trivialised her achievements. She said she kept seeing herself as 'fucked', and this made it hard for her to notice changes. When I talked with her about whether she thought she was ready to take any further steps in the new direction, she began to talk about her fears in relation to having to start a new life as a different sort of person if she went further with the changes. At this point, I restrained further changes. I invited her to keep track of any examples of occasions where she was being true to herself or valuing herself.

Sessions 7-10

When I enquired about the extent to which self-appreciation was evident in her life versus the extent of self-depreciation, Alice began to describe more examples of times when she had valued something about herself. I gathered a lot of details about these examples, and she then spontaneously recalled further occasions of self-appreciation. As this progressed, Alice noticed that she had started to break with her habit of being for others in friendships and of putting others' needs before her own:

> *The most important strategy for me was to acknowledge and leave behind contexts that continued to arouse and create pain.*
>
> *Once I was able to do this, I was able to construct new ways of interacting with people, in more positive and self-gratifying relationships. I didn't insist on maintaining relationships out of guilt or self-destruction, and saw the benefits of trusting people and establishing supportive relationships.* (1988)

At this point, she once again started to talk about her habit of bingeing and vomiting, saying that it was happening more often. I got some details about this by asking her about the effect bulimia had had on her life, and she was able to talk with me about some periods of her life where she had escaped bulimia, as well as about how she had achieved this (tracking unique outcomes). During this phase of therapy, Alice put me in the picture about further ways she had been in training to see herself as 'fucked' (e.g. significant upsetting interactions with her mother), and the ways in which she thought she had been affected by this training, e.g. hiding herself, fears of rejection if she was more herself, and seeing herself as being responsible for everything that has gone wrong in her life. I talked with her about the habit of bulimia being a way she could be less 'herself', and this was an idea she could connect with. I suggested she keep track of times where she refused bulimia's invitations (tracking unique outcomes).

Sessions 11-14

Alice began to have some victories over bulimia and, for the first time, to allocate more responsibility to family members for her distress. I explored these developments in detail, describing them as achievements in self-appreciation. I talked with her about her ideas about how bulimia had originally become so influential in her life. She identified the origin of many secret habits in her life, including bulimia, in response to the extreme reactions of her parents to her developing sexuality. I also asked her about things like, in what ways she thought she had subjected herself to fitting with ideal images for women in terms of shape. I enquired about whether she thought these images might further have encouraged her to be less than herself, and she agreed this may have been the case. We talked in detail about the occasions where she had beaten bulimia and, as sessions went on, she had more victories over it. In response to this, I asked her questions like: 'How do you think it was possible for you to allow yourself to be more fully yourself on that occasion?', 'How were you able to break away from subjecting yourself to society's prescriptions for thinness for women, and to appreciate yourself in this way?'

In some of my questions I was inviting her to identify the influence on her personally of the broader social context of patriarchy which supports the idea of women being less than themselves, or invalidating themselves. I was also inviting her to consider ways she had been for herself and had withstood these prescriptions.

Alice experienced a period of anxiety in response to the changes she was making. She talked about being worried about losing her 'old self' - who would she become? She also described her habit of picking at herself for the first time in more detail. We tracked the story about how this habit had become stronger recently. I was also able to locate some unique outcomes, or occasions where she had not given into the habit. However, Alice said she was unsure about whether she wanted to talk further about this habit. I asked her to consider the consequences of talking further about it in therapy.

Alice then began to recall some frightening situations which happened to her as a child at bedtime, and together we recognised how the picking habit had become an ally to fear. It had become a way to hypnotise herself and stop fear, and another way to 'lose herself'. I suggested that she schedule half an hour each night for this habit so that she might get more information about how it helped her with her fears. To use Alice's own words:

Upfront acknowledgement, and giving myself permission to include these [habits] in moderation, allowed me to change my perspective on these behaviours and slowly take control of them.

Alice was noticing, at this stage, that she was no longer letting her distress in any one area of her life overwhelm all the others, and that she experienced a sense of feeling more in control.

Sessions 14-20

It was clear that Alice was experiencing more control over her self-destructive habits. She recognised readily how she was able to stop herself from being taken over by them - our conversation contained more spontaneous examples from her about this, and less examples about being overwhelmed by the habits. She discovered many new strategies for handling her fears at night, e.g. by listening to music to help her relax.

The problem-saturated description was taking up less space in therapy, and Alice was constructing a new story for herself. When I explored how all this had been achieved, Alice said:

I've changed my ideology about myself. At first I thought, 'I'm fucked'. Then I moved on to thinking, 'They're fucked', about my family. Now I believe that I'm okay - I have my problems in life, but I am okay and I am healing myself.

She also said that she felt less anxious and worried about herself generally, and this meant that she had more space to deal with the self-destructive habits.

To encourage a performance of meaning around these numerous changes, I asked her about what difference this new view of herself was making to the way she treated herself day-to-day, what difference this made to her relationships with family and with friends, and about what new possibilities these changes might open up for her.

I predicted 'hiccups' with the habits, and we discussed how she might deal with them, e.g. scheduling in time for the picking habit.

Alice has maintained these changes, with bulimia and picking at herself almost disappearing from her life. She has formed new relationships in which she experiences caring and acknowledgement. She says she now believes she is competent and is actively achieving changes in her own life. She describes the experience of seeing herself in a context when problems occur, i.e. she no longer labels herself as a problem when things go wrong. She reports feeling good and valuing herself in the presence of people who have been problematic for her in the past. She has had some hiccups, but does not feel overwhelmed when they occur. She has made many steps, which she has drawn my attention to, in being more fully herself, in valuing herself, and in being less a person for others and more for herself.

I have stopped having regular sessions with Alice and have invited her to contact me if she wants to review things with me. I recently saw her when she experienced a hiccup in relation to the break-up of a relationship. She continues to experience a sense of control over her own life, e.g. recently she has come up with the idea of using her dreams as resources for herself.

I'm not perfect, I'm still self-critical and constantly striving for self-improvement - but I'm okay and I like myself and, despite my normal emotional ups and downs, I understand myself and my reactions and I

now feel in control and able to move on past the pain of my past.
(August 1988)

Conclusion

In conclusion, I believe that there are many unhelpful, limiting and potentially oppressive ideas being applied in the service of therapy with women who were sexually abused as children. My preference has been for a framework which acknowledges and accesses the influence of familial and relationship contexts (including the context of the woman's relationship with the man who abused her), as well as the influence of restraining ideas from patriarchal ideology, in the process of the development of problems in the woman's life. Therapy may be seen as an opportunity to address restraints or dominant stories, through the therapist assisting the woman to generate double descriptions or alternative stories; this allows the woman a chance to re-tell her story about herself. It has been my experience, in approaching therapy like this, that many women have responded by strongly challenging the dominant stories in creative ways, finding solutions which have been empowering for them.

Acknowledgements

I wish to thank Lesley Laing and Catherine Munro, who have each made particular and special contributions in helping me develop ideas which have been critical to the writing of this chapter. I am very grateful to both of them for their assistance with various drafts of the chapter, and for their invaluable support. I am grateful to Bronwyn Cintio for her assistance in the early stages of writing the chapter. Finally, I wish to thank Michael White for his encouraging comments about the chapter, and Steven Kamsler and Melanie Kamsler for their loving support.

Notes

1. First published 1990 in Durrant, M. & White, C. (eds), *Ideas for Therapy With Sexual Abuse.* Adelaide: Dulwich Centre Publications. Republished here with permission.

2. Amanda lives and works in Sydney, Australia, and has been exploring narrative ideas and practices for over ten years in the course of her work as a therapist. During

this time she has been refreshed and inspired by the experience of working alongside the people who meet with her as they discover untold possibilities in their personal and professional lives. She has also enjoyed the great conversations that have been unfolding through having the opportunity to offer presentations and workshops in Australia, New Zealand, Canada and USA. Amanda can be reached by phone or fax at (61-2) 9958 5418, and her email address is kamsler@ozemail.com.au

3. These are the definitions adopted by Dympna House.

4. I wish to acknowledge the original work of Lesley Laing, who was the instigator for ideas expressed in this section of the chapter.

5. I would like to acknowledge the valuable contribution of Catherine Munro, with whom I consulted at various stages of this process.

References

Blake-White, J. & Kline, C.M. 1985: 'Treating the dissociative process in adult victims of childhood incest.' *Social Casework,* September, pp.394-402.

Calvert, G. 1984: 'Letter to the Editor.' *Australian Journal of Family Therapy,* 5:1.

Deighton, J. & McPeek, P. 1985: 'Group treatment: Adult victims of child sexual abuse.' *Social Casework,* September, pp.403-410.

Durrant, M. 1987: 'Therapy with young people who have been the victims of sexual assault.' *Family Therapy Case Studies,* 2(1):57-63.

Ellenson, G. 1985: 'Detecting a history of incest: A predictive syndrome.' *Social Casework,* November, pp.525-532.

Faria, G. & Belohlavek, N. 1984: 'Treating female adult survivors of childhood incest.' *Social Casework,* October, pp.465-471.

Furniss, T. 1983: 'Family process in the treatment of intra-familial child sexual abuse.' *Journal of Family Therapy,* 5:263-278.

Gutheil, T. & Avery, N. 1977: 'Multiple overt incest as family defence against loss.' *Family Process,* pp.105-116.

Herman, J. 1985: 'Father-daughter incest.' In Burgess, A. (ed), *Rape & Sexual Assault - A Research Handbook.*

Justice, B. & Justice, R. 1979: *The Broken Taboo: Sex in the Family.* New York: Human Sciences Press.

Laing, L. & Kamsler, A. 1988: Training workshops for therapists working with women who were sexually abused in childhood. Sydney, Australia.

Lustig, N. et al. 1966: 'Incest: A family group survival pattern.' *Archives of General Psychiatry,* 14:31-40.

Machotka, P. et al. 1967: 'Incest as a family affair.' *Family Process,* 6:98-116.

McCarthy, I.D. & Byrne, N.O. 1988: 'Mis-taken love: Conversations on the problem of incest in an Irish context.' *Family Process,* 27(2):181-199.

Munro, C. 1989: 'White and the cybernetic therapies: News of difference.' *Australian & New Zealand Journal of Family Therapy,* 8(4):183-192.

O'Donnell, C. & Craney, J. 1982: 'Incest and the reproduction of the patriarchal family.' In O'Donnell, C. & Craney, J. (eds), *Family Violence in Australia.* Cheshire: Longman.

Shapiro, S. 1987: 'Self-mutilation and self-blame in incest victims.' *American Journal of Psychotherapy,* 41(1):46-54.

Tomm, K. 1989: 'Externalizing the problem and internalizing personal agency.' *Journal of Strategic & Systemic Therapies,* 8:1.

Tsai, M. et al. 1979: 'Childhood molestations: Psychological functioning in adult women.' *Journal of Abnormal Psychology,* 88:407-417.

Waldby, C. 1987: 'Theoretical perspectives on incest: A survey of the literature in breaking the silence.' *Breaking the Silence: A report based upon the findings of the Women Against Incest Phone-in Survey (Sydney 1984).* Haberfield, Australia: Dympna House.

Ward, E. 1984: *Father-Daughter Rape.* London: The Women's Press.

White, M. 1986: 'Negative explanation, restraint & double description: A template for family therapy.' *Family Process,* 25(2):169-184.

White, M. 1986: 'Anorexia nervosa: A cybernetic perspective.' In Elka-Harkaway, J. (ed), *Eating Disorders.* Maryland: Aspen Publishers.

White, M. 1988: 'The process of questioning: A therapy of literary merit?' *Dulwich Centre Newsletter,* Winter.

White, M. 1988-89: 'The externalizing of the problem.' *Dulwich Centre Newsletter,* Summer.

White, M. & Epston, D. 1989: *Literate Means to Therapeutic Ends.* Adelaide: Dulwich Centre Publications. (Also published as White, M. & Epston, D. 1990: *Narrative Means to Therapeutic Ends.* New York: Norton.)

5

Sarah-Jane's Story[1]

by

Loretta Perry[2]

This is Sarah-Jane's story. Sarah-Jane is twenty-nine years old and lives with a brain that she says often trips her up (some people might call this autism). Sarah-Jane's brain often disappears conversations, freezes gestures, magnifies worldly concerns, transfixes intentions, and promises her invisibility when visibility seems ominous. Sarah-Jane has been exposed to many treatments and cures - from psychiatry to psychotropic medication, and has undergone many assessments that often seem to vanish into the ether.

Sarah-Jane and Loretta met one another because 'the spitting thing (constant hacking and spitting) in Sarah-Jane's life was 'freaking people out', and preventing her from going out into the world. It seemed that 'the spitting thing' was joining forces with existent trickery and was having overwhelming success in hiding Sarah-Jane away from the world. As time passed, other sources of concern were also revealed, including 'scratching', 'closing people out', and the fact that Sarah-Jane's brain hasn't permitted her to eat at all during the day for five years and has closely monitored her attempts at night-food.

Sarah-Jane and Loretta decided to try and record a part of Sarah-Jane's story through extracts from letters that have documented their conversations over the last eight months. Sarah-Jane's brain prevents her from reading and from most writing but, in spite of this, she can fluently record her name and loves to write when letters are sounded out for her. Sarah-Jane also insists that letters are read to her, and this paper has been read to her four times already.

Hi Sarah-Jane,

It was great to meet you today and have all the conversations we did. I particularly noticed how you're able to do a couple of things at the same time. I also noticed the way you like to think for a while about things we talk of before you answer.

Sarah-Jane, you said today that 'this fear thing' makes you: *think some bad things about yourself; feel some bad things about yourself; do spitting things; stop swallowing properly; stop eating like you'd like to eat; stop making friends; stay at home more than you'd like to stay at home; give up control over your own life; think that fear is in control of your life;* and you said that it *makes other people not know what to do when spitting starts.*

Sarah-Jane, this is one heck of a bossy problem. What do you think?

One of the things that you said about 'this fear thing' was that 'it is sometimes in charge of you but at other times you are in charge of it'. You also said that 'it was interesting for you to know that you can be in charge of *this fear thing*'. You said that you want to get back 'in charge' of your life. You said that 'in charge' wants you to: *do more things by yourself; not get tense; talk about this fear thing like we did today; remind yourself that you're* in charge; *tell* this fear thing *to 'GO AWAY' as soon as it starts; notice more when* this fear thing *and* the spitting thing *go away; and notice what you're doing when it's gone away - notice what's different.*

This is a lot to put up against the bossy problem of 'this fear thing' don't you think? Are there any other things that might help?

I got a bit excited hearing you tell Joanie (Sarah-Jane's Mum) about your discovery of wanting to be 'in charge' of 'this fear thing'. I was also excited that today you noticed that 'this fear thing' only stopped you from swallowing a few times. How come 'this fear thing' only stopped you from swallowing a few times today? Do you have any ideas?

Sarah-Jane, you also said that you could keep eye contact today. I didn't know that sometimes something takes eye contact away from you. What robs you of eye contact do you think? Do you have any ideas?

It was great to meet you and I'm glad that you liked my house. Please phone me during the week and let me know how 'in charge' is doing.

Loretta.

Dear Sarah-Jane,

You said today that during the past week you felt 'a bit more in charge of things'. Does this mean that your brain has been winning this week? Was there a time this week when 'this fear thing' almost had you spitting but didn't? How come?

Sarah-Jane, I was wondering whether you could see how Joanie and I might be surprised that you made such a big effort to be 'in charge' this week because we know how long 'this fear thing.' has been around. What do you think is the most surprising to you, Joanie and me?

On Saturday you described how big 'this fear thing' is by drawing it like this:

And you drew the size of 'in charge' like this:

What sorts of things might grow 'in charge' up so that it gets bigger than 'this fear thing'?

One of the most fascinating things for me that we talked about today was about how questions and conversations 'get lost in your brain'. You told me that when I ask you a question that 'it goes into your brain and sometimes an answer comes out, but sometimes the question gets lost in there'. You also said that 'it is important for you to answer but sometimes it is hard because the questions get lost'. I'll be interested to know more about this.

The other interesting thing we talked about today was the scratching of your arms and legs, do you remember? Sarah-Jane, you said that scratching was more for 'hurting yourself' and less for 'caring about yourself'. I'd be interested to know about the times that 'caring for yourself' stops you from scratching yourself. I look forward to talking more next week.

Loretta.

Dear Sarah-Jane,

This is just a little letter, 'cause on Saturday some of my questions got swallowed up by the part of your brain that doesn't always respond to questions. I noticed that a lot of my questions got lost somewhere. Did you notice that? What is different between the times that questions can be answered and the times when questions get lost somewhere? When you listen to the walkman does this interfere with questions being answered by you do you think? Does the walkman block out people's questions? Are questions and answers necessary to make conversation? What happens to conversations, do you think, when questions get lost? Is it more for stopping conversation or more for keeping them going?

I'm really appreciating your ability to tell me what needs to happen on Saturday when we spend time together. Is talking for one hour or more on Saturday too long do you think? Anyway, as usual, lots of questions Sarah-Jane. I'm also interested in the answers to these so that we can keep on making conversations!

Loretta.

Dear Sarah-Jane,

Some of the most exciting and surprising things for me on Saturday were when you said that 'in charge' wanted you to say and do the following things:
- *that you'd be willing to take a risk and ask me to massage you,*
- *that you would try swallowing the saliva rather than spitting it out,*
- *that you'd like to be more independent,*
- *that you're ready to sit down with your family and have a conversation with them.*

How come fear didn't stop you from trying to do all these things?! Are you sure that you're not going too fast? What makes you think that you are going at the right pace? I recall you saying, 'I think it will help me'.

We also talked about happiness. When I asked you about whether you were happy two weeks ago, you drew happiness and said it was like this:

Then you drew happiness like this for last week:
Sarah-Jane you said that you'd like happiness to grow even bigger, as big as this:

Do you have some ideas about how to let happiness into your life? Who would you like to tell about this happiness? I was wondering what other people in your family were noticing about you lately, have you asked them? Are you like a new Sarah-Jane to them do you think? Is the new Sarah-Jane taking some risks in her life? How else would you like to surprise them? Can you ask them and tell me next week when I see you? Could you ask your family to make a list of the things they've noticed you being more able to do recently?

Loretta.

Dear Sarah-Jane,

It's been a long time since I've written to you and I'm a couple of ideas behind. I'm sorry about last week, I was a bit sick with the flu. I managed, however, to check out some work for you - it's okay for Burnside where I work for you to come one day a week and do some work there yourself. [Burnside took a chance, as it often does, to offer Sarah-Jane a place in the agency, hoping that this would make a difference.] You could copy letters, do some typing, play music, and meet some of the young people who come in there. What do you think? Let's talk about your readiness to work. Is there anything you need in particular to be thinking about to prepare yourself to go to work? What do you think? You said that you felt it important to tell people who already work there some things about yourself such as:

- *that you'd like people not to be anxious about spitting if you spit,*

- *that you're trying to come out into the world more and need some help,*

- *that you'd like people to keep trying to talk to you even if you don't answer.*

I was interested to hear you telling me on Saturday about the spitting thing being controlled by thoughts that now tell it to 'swallow' instead of 'cough up'. We didn't continue talking about this for some reason. Can we talk about it more next week?

Loretta.

Dear Sarah-Jane,

Today you said something that has stuck in my mind. You said, 'I'm getting there, slowly but surely'. This got me thinking about, of all things, turtles. Have you ever seen one? Turtles warn against pushing ahead too fast. Turtles, if given opportunities, can only progress at their own speed. I was wondering Sarah-Jane if, like a turtle, you felt that your achievements - going to work, having a massage and acupuncture, going to aerobics and maintaining eye contact (to name but a few) - are keeping up with the speed you're wanting to go in this life of yours? Are you moving ahead too fast? What do you think? What are some of the other things you're involved in that cause you to think that you're progressing in life in the way that you want for yourself?

Did you know Sarah-Jane that turtles bury their eggs in the ground? Baby turtles rely on the sun to birth them. Sarah-Jane, I was just wondering whether some of your ideas get buried just like turtle eggs - are they snug and cared for in your brain, waiting for opportunities to bring them to life? Can you think of an occasion this week where an idea - something that you have been thinking of for a while - managed to break free, just like the baby turtles do at birth?

You know how the sun hatches baby turtles Sarah-Jane, does talking to people, and people constantly talking to you (never giving up on talking to you), eventually hatch your ideas and abilities? Are people a bit like the sun in your life - getting you warmed up to your own ideas about yourself, until you can birth them one at a time? Can you still remember the times when new people coming into your life used to be so scary for you? How come you now welcome new people into your life? What's got you ready for new people like Iris, Helen, Anne, Damien, Trish, Jonathon, Colleen and Lyn in your life? How come you've been able to let all of these people befriend you? What might they see in you that would cause them all to want to be in your life?

I wanted to tell you another story. You know how turtles sometimes fall over - their shells ending up on the ground with their legs sticking straight up in the air? Given their heavy shells, given the heavy loads they have to carry, do you reckon that they could easily right themselves? Or would we expect that it takes a bit of time for them to right themselves? Sarah-Jane, do you think your struggle is a bit like that of the turtle with a heavy load? What sorts of experiences are still tough for you Sarah-Jane? Can you name one? What sorts of things are going to take some time to right themselves in the ways that you'd like? Can you name some of these experiences?

Can you also tell me more about the things you've achieved in spite of struggle - you know that long list of achievements? Sarah-Jane, I was wondering how come struggle continues to win over defeat?

Loretta.

PS. I was wondering Sarah-Jane whether next Saturday you'd be ready to go to a restaurant with me? We could go for 10 minutes and sit outside on the footpath - you know the restaurant next to my place. What do you think? What would you need to take with you so that you'd feel safe to do this? Anyway I'll leave it up to you and we can talk about it on Saturday.

Dear Sarah-Jane,

I was talking to Joanie today out on your sunroof. This provided me with an opportunity to reflect on some of the times we've shared. Would you be interested to re-hear how time for me with you has a way of moving through dark and light, through laughter and intensity, through chambers of talk and silence, through musical wounds and threads of pleasure, slippery connections and joy, awesome and infectious!

Sarah-Jane, there are so many shared times that I don't know where to begin. Consulting with you has included times of communicating with you through talking pens, radio stations playing simultaneously, pocket televisions with miniature characters acting out, watches that speak out the time at the touch of a button, a guitar that insists on constant tuning, an aggressive walkman and a threatened banjo. I've often puzzled at the way your brain can listen to several competing voices - Sarah-Jane, in what ways is it still helpful to listen through musical filters?

What about the day you dropped onto the floor ready to be massaged - the first time you had asked to be touched. I have to tell you Sarah-Jane, I got a shock. It took me by surprise, so much so that I didn't know what to do for a moment. I remember you explained your newfound ability simply by saying that you were ready to let someone touch you.

And Sarah-Jane, what about the time you went with your sister, Amy, to buy some trendy clothes - those tight purple velvet pants and jacket?! I remember you looking very groovy with your mascaraed lashes setting out for a coffee in a local café. This was the beginning of us taking Glebe by surprise. What about our Market Therapy - the consultations in the market place? Or the time we went to that posh restaurant at Watson's Bay and we sat at the table as you upended endless cups of coffee. I am thinking of the way you've taken to sipping coffee and tea. The way you wet your lips with the liquid and reject the minutest drop should it pass your lips! And I have noticed how self-care is now alive and well. You now get carried around by legs that self-care look after, not self-harm that used to have you taking pieces out of them. How have you managed to gain even more weight, and remember Sarah-Jane, you've come up from 38 kilos, in spite of your brain not allowing you to eat during the day? When did self-care get a grip on your life? Did it happen overnight, did it creep up on you, or is it one of the effects of a hard-won struggle for you? Which one is it Sarah-Jane?

The thing I most want to ask is, where has the spitting and choking gone? Sarah-Jane, when you first came to work two months ago, you arrived with much fear, timidity and a flurry of spluttering, here, there, and everywhere. Do you remember - spluttering, spitting and choking were all there, no holds barred, in those days? So where, Sarah-Jane, has it all gone to? Spitting used to use up half a box of tissues and these days gets away with only a couple. Has work scared it off? Are you too busy to spare a moment to pay it any attention, let alone give it any time, particularly now that you are learning how to be in the workplace? I know it can make a comeback, but where on earth does it go when it disappears? Have you got a trick or two up your sleeve to disappear it?

Recently I've been hearing about so many good things that have been happening for you Sarah-Jane. Iris tells me that at work you've changed from staying put in an office to getting about with her, to volunteering introductions of yourself, to wandering over to where the young people hang out and joining them to listen to music, to independently taking on some work tasks, to phoning up people to talk to, to sharing the idea of a cup of tea, to wanting to abandon work to dance the morning away with the young people! Iris tells me that you are coming out of isolation and are wanting to join in with what's happening around you. She tells me that what she most appreciates about you is that you've brought joy with you to the workplace and that this joy is catching.

I've also heard from Joanie about some new steps. She told me that last week you popped out for a couple of hours by yourself from midnight to two in the morning for a bit of late-night shopping. She also told me that she was shocked that you bought some flowers for the first time to put in your room and that you'd like to go on a camp with other people! Well stone the crows! What can I say? Where are these ideas coming from? How much of your life is now outside of your room defying the part of your brain that has wanted a commitment to a room-bound life?

Now that you're more becoming a woman in your own right Sarah-Jane, with increasing mobility in the world, how do you think you can both grow yourself as an individual as well as ensure your safety? Is safety a concern for you, particularly now that your brain might be wanting you to both eat during the night as well as go shopping for food? What plans has it got in mind for you? Do you know or do they come as a surprise to you too? What do you know about yourself that leads you to believe that being in charge of your life also causes you to be able to ensure your safety?

Sorry this is such a long letter - but so much seems to be happening!

Loretta

Sarah-Jane came into my life eight months ago to remind me that within this world there are a multitude of formulas for survival, life, and magic, not just one. Sarah-Jane, her family, and our workplace, remind me of the need for tenacity, of the possibility of building on dreams, and of the power of belonging. They also remind me of the stories of my own life, my own belonging.

They remind me of the narrow definitions of who we are 'supposed to be', and of the struggles and joys of living in waters far beyond the mainstream.[3] Sarah-Jane's story feels like a celebration - of her own talents and abilities, of those of the other people in her life, of small steps, and of the work that is community.

I think that our community has been powerful because, individually, the people concerned (and there are many more than I've been able to mention) can either remember struggles in their own lives, or continue to try to imagine what it's like to walk in the shoes of Sarah-Jane. This has demanded much from us all. At times it has tested our compassion and stretched our collective abilities to care, teach, love, and share.

Sarah-Jane has presented us all with innumerable behaviours to both comprehend and accept, some of which have stopped our hearts for a moment or two. In reflecting upon some of the more difficult times in working with Sarah-Jane, I'd have to say that the times that are the most confronting have little to do with what Sarah-Jane is doing and more to do with what I have the potential to do myself. The times that are most confronting are the times when I can contribute to the creation of 'other', the times when I am tempted to feel bad or shamed by Sarah-Jane's behaviours - by her spitting, staring, hiding, repetitive talking, unpredictability, her responses to will and desire, and their frequent chaotic consequences.

These behaviours when they occur, particularly in new situations or when we are out and about together, sometimes get transformed through the eyes of others until they come to reflect my own 'disability' as opposed to my own 'weirdly abled' talents (a term regularly used by David Epston). I have the potential in these situations to feel that there is indeed something wrong with me or with Sarah-Jane - and if it's not me then it's got to be Sarah-Jane.

Sarah-Jane has taught me that I too have fallen prey to this kind of societal process, this invitation to blame, shame and/or stigmatise. My times with Sarah-Jane have taught me that, like issues of race and class, the language and conversations in relation to disability are institutionalised in the fabric of our culture. To name them and confront them in myself causes me pain as well as joy. I am confident that these ideas and feelings are not unique to me, that they are shared by all the people in Sarah-Jane's work team.

In saying this, I don't want to detract from, or minimise, the hard work of team-work or the daily time-consuming grind. I'd like to pay homage to Iris who leads the work team at Burnside. Iris has a Doctorate in Weirdly Abled Work (she's worked with me for three years!). Burnside extended an opportunity to Sarah-Jane, so tiny an opportunity in the overall scheme of things, but so significant for Sarah-Jane, that I think it will have life-long ripples. It is always my hope in agency work that together we hold a belief that 'she ain't heavy, she's my sister'.

Finally, I'd like somehow to reflect the significance to this story of Sarah-Jane's family, her mum Joanie, and dad Kevin, and her nine siblings. I have no way of expressing what it has meant to me to witness what seems to be their unrelenting belief in their daughter and sister. I have no way of fully comprehending their day-to-day experience of life and love with Sarah-Jane and what their support has meant. And I have no way of adequately acknowledging the significance of them trusting us with Sarah-Jane. Without this trust we would never have had the opportunity to learn all that we have learned from Sarah-Jane and, as Iris says, 'we would never have had the opportunity to catch a little bit of her joy'.

Acknowledgements

Sarah-Jane and Loretta would like to acknowledge the parts played in this story by Joanie, Tim, Dad, Amy, Jenny, Iris, Helen, Anne, Damien, Trish, Jonathon, Colleen, Lyn and the organisation of Burnside.

Notes

1. First published in the 1997 No.4 issue of the *Dulwich Centre Newsletter*. Republished here with permission.

2. There have been several people in my life that, during times of distress, spoke words so wondrous and magical that the effects of their music changed the course of

history. Their contributions to my ideas and the multi-directions I have pursued in life have caused me to experience the magnificence of a humble journey. My desire is always to follow in the tradition of music-makers where creativity, synchronicity, hopes - lost and found, and reciprocity, is taken for granted. And from this place, I can begin ...

Loretta can be contacted at Dulwich Centre, 345 Carrington Street, Adelaide 5000, South Australia.

3. If you'd like to read more about Loretta's heritage, you might be interested in her paper: 'Against the grain', in White, C. & Hales, J. (1997), *The Personal is the Professional: Therapists Reflect on Their Families, Lives and Work.* Adelaide: Dulwich Centre Publications.

PART III

Working
with
Groups

6

Busting Out - Breaking Free
A group program for young women wanting to reclaim their lives from anorexia nervosa[1]
by[2]
Marilyn Kraner & Kate Ingram

It makes you think you have full control over your life. You think you have control, but the only thing you have control over is eating. But suddenly you don't even have control over that, you can make no decisions about your own life, it is fully taken over by others because they deem that you are too irrational to make any of your own decisions or do anything and anything that comes from your mouth is either ignored or is believed as being total crap. (Extract from a story written by a fourteen-year-old young woman about her experience of hospitalisation for her refusal to eat.)

Dominant psychological and psychiatric conceptualisations of anorexia nervosa often define it as a personal and internal maladjustment (MacSween 1993). As a result, sufferers can be treated as passive recipients of psychological and physiological treatment (Tanzer 1997). This view emphasises the ingestion of food and weight gain as primary goals for intervention. And yet, as the opening quote suggests, the experience of anorexia seems more relevantly located in the social domain of interaction, where food and weight are imbued with meanings about control, personal agency and tension. It is our view that anorexia sits at the intersection between the physical body and how that body is perceived and experienced.

The concept of an intersection offers an interesting metaphor with which to summarise what we learnt from our experiences in developing a narrative-based group program for young women diagnosed with anorexia nervosa.

Firstly, an intersection has a number of different approaches. The program elicited and utilised the experiences of the young women themselves, and the views of parents and interpretations of those professionals attempting to help them. Secondly, intersections provide the opportunity for a change in direction. Throughout the program, we were challenged by the young women to remain open to changes in direction as a result of adopting the position that young people should participate in the design of interventions which involve them. Finally, intersections can be the sites of collision and inevitably should be entered with caution, seeking to first learn what is on the other paths. Anorexia requires the consideration of a number of key issues: the construct of gender within the identity formation of young women; the balance between care and control of children and young people within families by adults; and the inadvertent promotion of values of helplessness and dependence by helping institutions.

In this paper, we will describe the process of establishing a group program for young women diagnosed with anorexia nervosa, which was established in the context of an outpatient child and adolescent psychiatry service attached to a metropolitan public hospital. We will explore the strategies used to promote opportunities for reflection by the young women participating in the program, and identify the key outcomes for the young women. Along the way, we also present views expressed by the young women about the experiences of anorexia, and the processes designed to help them. These are significant commentaries about the current practices of mental health services in responding to the needs of young women diagnosed with anorexia nervosa. We also document our reflections on the experiences of facilitating the program.

It is important to note that, throughout this paper, we are not aiming to criticise individual professionals, but rather the particular conceptions and practices of the health professions which by their nature deny patients the opportunity to exercise personal agency and control. Indeed, as health professionals ourselves, we acknowledge the difficulty of stepping outside the dominant health discourses to reflect on practice. We are also part of this system of beliefs.

The consultation phase

The criteria for the program was that participants in the group were or had previously been hospitalised as a result of their eating difficulties. The group consisted of five young women aged between fourteen and seventeen years who were referred from the medical and psychiatric sections of the hospital. The group met each week for eleven weeks.

An initial meeting was held with the young women in order to seek their input about the content of the sessions. We hoped not only to learn about their opinions but to establish an environment which promoted openness and a genuine sense of collaboration. Through a combination of questionnaires, interviews and a group consultancy session, we were able to access the experiences of these young women and their families with the health and psychiatric systems. We explored ideas about possible topics that could be incorporated into the program and considered ways of involving the parents.

These discussions highlighted how, in some circumstances for these young women and at times ourselves, the mainstream health systems act to imprison rather than liberate. Intervention strategies such as bed-rest, isolating them from others on the unit, linking certain privileges to weight gain, and forcing them to sit with a staff member after each meal, were experienced by the young women as restricting their capacities to control anorexia on their own. As a result, we adopted an empowerment model for the group encouraging the participants to share in the responsibility of directing the group.

The comments reported in this paper are those made by the young women who took part in the program and their parents. Whilst the young women have given their permission for us to share their feelings, they expressed apprehension about the possible reactions of readers. We hope that you as the reader respect their courage to be so open about their lives and we invite you to respond if you wish. We have kept the young women and parents anonymous at their request.

Running the group

In this section, we outline in detail the areas of activity and interest which directed the evolution of the program and include comments from the participants.

Story-telling

The group began with the use of personal as well as fictional stories. Excerpts from stories including: 'The Ugly Duckling' and 'Women who Run with the Wolves' (Estes 1992); as well as Aboriginal tales such as 'How the Sun Came to Be', were read and discussed briefly at the start of each group. We chose these stories for a variety of reasons including our simple enjoyment of them. In addition, however, each story acted as a metaphor for us promoting messages that we felt were important in our lives, such as people's ability to stand up for their rights and overcome adversity, the power of the group process, and the importance and strength of women. We hoped to share these experiences with the group.

We believed that these narratives allowed the participants to explore more freely their feelings and ideas. We found that storytelling and its focus on the use of metaphors promoted active participation through encouraging the young women to engage with the messages of each story. The meaning they ascribed to each story varied according to the unique experience of each young woman. In this way, we believed that the group quickly moved into accepting a level of analysis which was both personal and collective. It included the reflection of each participant and facilitator as we reacted to the relevance of the stories in our lives. This process encouraged discussion and generated a supportive environment for the group.

Establishing an identity outside of anorexia nervosa: the negativity monster as a worthy opponent

We drew on the concept of 'externalizing the problem' (White & Epston 1989; White 1989; Epston 1993) to begin a process which firstly marked out the physical, emotional and psychological effects of not eating, and then provided the space to develop a more preferred way of being for the young women.

Rather than continue to blame themselves for being 'anorexic', the group was encouraged to blame 'anorexia' and its practices. As a way of externalizing the problem we used the film *Ghostbusters* (1984). In one segment of the movie, a main character becomes possessed by a ghost and finds herself acting, speaking and thinking in ways she might otherwise not have. Her whole personality appears to alter. She becomes a tool for the ghost's desires and ambitions.

The young women in the group identified with the character's experiences in *Ghostbusters*. They spoke of their lives being invaded by anorexia much as the woman had been possessed by the ghost. They spoke of their lives being transformed and their identities altered by anorexia. Through discussion, the group agreed that they viewed the effects of anorexia as negative and controlling. Participants named their experience and chose to describe their struggle with anorexia as a 'battle with the negativity monster'. We then were able to explore in greater detail the impact of the negativity monster on their lives and relationships.

Creating an alternative history with the voice of pioneers

Early in the group process, we introduced the work of the Anti-Anorexia League developed by David Epston. The Anti-Anorexia League is made up of a group of people diagnosed with anorexia. They have gathered stories that support, inform, and inspire others in their battle against anorexia. The League could be described as a collection of expert knowledges (Epston & White 1992).

The 'League's Archives' enabled us to introduce the self-narratives of others who had protested against the effects of anorexia nervosa. Through these stories, our group heard how others had unmasked anorexia's purposes, its betrayals and lies. We believe that this process enabled the group to build a sense of its own identity based on an alternative history of the treatment of anorexia. The League confirmed the existence of pioneers who have been willing to challenge the value-base inherent in the traditional conceptualisations of anorexia and its associated treatment.

Group members were invited to explore their feelings related to their experiences and began to gain confidence to be able to tell their own stories. The group validated each of the stories with patient listening and attention. The audience (the others in the group including ourselves) were important in not only hearing and acknowledging the old story, but later as witnesses to the new preferred stories which emerged. Here is one young woman's story expressed at this point in the group.

I was nothing, nothing in a nothing world, a nothing living a nothing life. I didn't matter, nothing mattered!

My mother would call my name but she didn't mean me. She couldn't, for my name was no longer my identity, as identity to me meant nothing. Even my mother who conceived and gave birth to me meant nothing, as love does not exist in this nothing world of mine.

My world was that of pain. And pain to me was the only thing that didn't mean nothing. Pain was clear to me. I saw its haunting eyes staring me directly in the face - its pupils almost touching mine.

And because I didn't persist in defeating this pain, it defeated me. It grew until it became the monster that ruled my life, feeding itself off my weaknesses.

This pain, unknowingly at the time had become the only comfort which I could feel secure with. This comfort tricked me into believing it was my friend, tricking me into focussing all my thoughts and attentions towards its ungodly self.

I hated it! I hated its presence. I hated the everlasting battles that it would somehow manoeuvre into my brain. Yet it was my friend and at the time I didn't notice the influence it had over me, and to be disloyal would be a betrayal towards my one and only true friend. I couldn't separate myself from it and we became one.

We shut out all other beings for privacy. We didn't appreciate any individual invading what little space we had. We did not communicate or socialise with others, and we dared not let a piece of ourselves be revealed as this would mean others had the power to control and have power over our life.

This is how we would have liked to stay. Yet it didn't! Others soon forced their way into our life, always taking a piece of us with them and continuing to come back for more.

Recognising the impact of the negativity monster

We sought to find ways that might help turn their voice of victimhood into a voice of protest. We sought ways to reinforce their ability to see themselves separately from the 'monster' and in a more positive and stronger light.

The types of questions we used were:

- *What is the impact of the monster on your life and on your relationships with family and friends?*
- *What does the monster require you to do in order for it to survive?*
- *In what ways has the monster drafted others into believing they need to take control of your life?*

The impact of the negativity monster on the lives of the young women was viewed by them as extreme. We learnt from them that:

The anorexia makes promises:

... The monster says, 'the more you lose the more you'll have control' but the more I lose weight the more I end up in hospital without any control ...

... The monster promises that I will have more friends, that I'll become popular and my friends will look up to me ...

... It [the monster] assures me that if I lose weight my family will love and care for me more and I'll become special in their lives ...

The anorexia plays tricks:

... The monster tricks me into believing it is my one and only friend and that I should only listen to its messages ...

... Tricks me into believing that I will never be sick or die, that it won't happen to me even though everyone around me says I'm on death's door ...

... Fools me into believing that I am eating more than I actually am so that I say to myself, 'How could I have lost the weight when I'm eating so much'...

The anorexia imprisons:

... The monster makes me feel different to everyone else and encourages me to spend less and less time with people until I find myself all alone with the monster ...

... The monster doesn't give me a moment's break; it constantly makes me think about what I've eaten, what laxatives I've used and how much exercise I've done. It makes me obsessed ...

... The monster said [at the beginning] *that if I lose weight I'll get others to envy me ... that I can lose weight better than them ... in that way I can get back at them for using me. It really enjoys seeing me in competition with others and encourages me to compare myself all the time. I think it wants me to be jealous ...*

The anorexia controls emotions:

... When I lose weight the monster makes me feel good, happy with myself like I've achieved something; like I've got one over them [the enemy]; *they haven't beaten me* [the monster speaking] *...*

... The monster says that I shouldn't show my feelings, that I shouldn't let anyone in ...

.... Makes me feel depressed and often makes me hate myself ...

The anorexia controls relationships:

... When the monster is in charge others see me as irrational and make decisions for me as if I'm not there; as if I'm invisible ...

... The monster tricks me into believing that everyone but it is against me. That my parents, the doctors, dietitians, therapists are all my enemies and can't be trusted ...

... When the monster is strong others see me as not trying. They say I'm just being stubborn and believe that I'm really in control at the time I feel least in control ...

Hearing of the experiences of the others in the group and identifying the impact of the monster on their lives enabled the participants to separate themselves from the monster. They came to view the monster as an identity imposed on them rather than as a part of them. They no longer had to *be* the monster, and as such could have greater authority in controlling and changing its influence in their lives. It appeared that none of the young women wanted to continue to submit to the claims the monster held over their lives, and seemed attracted to the idea of challenging the monster. They moved into a position to use other aspects of their selves to fight the negativity monster. This is vividly captured by the following story written by a young woman in the group.

My Monster

Trapped, motionlessly inside my own thoughts. Tricked into believing what is right and wrong. Surely this is not my ideal life, being ruled by a monster more powerful than any other thought. The total power and control this monster creates is unknown to outsiders, but not to me. It can't hide from me, nor can I from it. It hovers around day and night always present, whether visible or not. It's like being trapped in a cubicle made of glass. You can see life, see that it does exist, friends, fun, excitement, it is all very visible and real, but this monster refuses to let me touch any of it, only looking no touching. But the glass cubicle, I'm locked in. I can see out but no-one else can see in. Just me and my monster all alone confiding in one another. I wish he would leave, I wait patiently for the day that he will give up and haunt someone else. Why did he choose me? Was I really that vulnerable and susceptible to his words? I argue constantly with him. I never give in without a fight. Sometimes when he is feeling weak, I win. At other times he is much too strong for me to even argue with for I know he will often come out on top. But when I do win on those odd occasions, I feel like a little part of him dies, he becomes a little weaker, but he is still there whispering things to me. He will leave, I am positive. It will be one hell of a battle, but I am just as strong as him and there is no way I will let him win!!

Strategies for fighting the monster

After considering the impact of the monster on the lives of these young women, we explored strategies for fighting the monster. We chose to do this by encouraging conversations about times when the young people had in the past protested or refused to co-operate with the requirements of the monster. In focusing on these experiences, we hoped to highlight the personal qualities and attributes they had utilised in achieving a position of dissent against the monster. This process is associated with White's concept of unique outcomes (White 1991).

In addition to exploring their fight against the monster, group participants were asked to think about the strengths and qualities that they had used previously to overcome other obstacles that they may have forgotten or not recognised. This seemed particularly helpful when a participant was unable to find many examples of her fight against the monster. By considering other seemingly non-related achievements and the personal qualities and skills used to accomplish these, they were encouraged to translate such characteristics to their fight against the negativity monster. The use of peer feedback was helpful in emphasising successes and drawing out personal attributes.

Here are some of the responses of the young women in relation to their fight against the negativity monster:

> *... Motivation to fight comes from being not able to do anything ... unable to go to parties; feeling like you are missing out ...*

> *... It's like I have two voices going in my head and they are arguing about whether or not I should eat. When I'm feeling really determined, really positive about myself, the voice wanting to fight against the monster is really powerful ...*

> *... Sometimes I can get really strong. That's when I have hope. Hope gives me strength. I look forward to going to school, going home, doing things I haven't done for ages ...*

> *... So to start off you might eat a little more at lunchtime but then you feel guilty and eat nothing for the next few meals ... the guilt is that strong. What helps me at these times is spending time with my friends and giving myself permission to be myself ...*

... Remembering what the monster takes away from you can be really useful.
I remember that the monster takes control away and gives others the power
to make decisions about me ...

Although the group members were able to recognise helpful strategies
from the past they might use now to reclaim their lives from the monster, they
appeared to find it difficult to do so. They struggled to identify occasions when
they may have been successful in weakening the monster, even if in a tiny way.
On reflection, we thought that perhaps we had moved to challenge the monster
before the young women had thoroughly explored the impact of anorexia on
their lives. This, we believe, may have been influenced by our desire to follow
our perception of what was important in a narrative approach, in this case the
need to find unique outcomes, rather than being aware of group process and
listening to what the young women were telling us.

The young women also noted that the monster continued to strongly
drive the group towards competition, encouraging self-comparison with others.
Perhaps more individual work prior to the group might have influenced this
rivalry and should have been considered. The lesson we learnt from this process
was to place more emphasis on the timing of the young women rather than our
own.

Addressing the political

Having focused on understanding the individual experience of anorexia
nervosa, we believed it to be important to contextualise these stories. We hoped
this process, which we have called 'addressing the political', would assist to
shift the understanding of this 'disorder' from a psychiatric phenomena which
defines individuals in terms of personal inadequacies, to considering anorexia
as a consequence of a socio-cultural narrative aimed at the oppression of
women.

We set out to provide an opportunity for the group to talk about and
examine those socially prevalent stories which shape and define women's
identities by manipulating their bodies. We sought to analyse the context of
women's experiences by considering the relationship between gender
construction, culture and the media. Our second aim was to explore how the

dominant practices of the health professions have helped to dislocate anorexia from its social dimensions and base its treatment in terms of personal/ psychological deficit.

Exploring gender, culture and the media

After hearing about the tyranny of power that the negativity monster appeared to exert on the lives of the young women, parallels between these individual experiences and the experiences of women became a matter of curiosity for us. Our life experience has led us to believe that, like the monster, our culture seeks to define, restrict and ultimately control the lives of women. Social practices appear to minimise, if not disregard, ideas based on intuition, emotion, compassion and other such qualities often labelled as feminine. Instead the logical, economic, rational take precedence. In addition, as women we are constantly bombarded with messages from the media about how we should look, behave, what we should buy, and what we need to do to be the perfect daughter, wife, mother, lover and employee.

The more we learnt about the practices of anorexia which appeared to feed on constant denial, self-regulation and conformity to a popular view of women as thin, lovable, gentle and subservient, it became apparent that these young women were indeed upholding many of our cultural messages about how women should be. It appeared to us that these young women had adopted the norms and requirements of our society only to find themselves being blamed, punished and ostracised for doing so.

From this thinking, we were curious to know whether the stories we held about this socio-cultural oppression of women were relevant to the experiences of the young women in the group.

We asked them the following questions:

- *Did they believe anorexia strikes down primarily women and, if so, why?*
- *Was there was a connection between society's expectations of women and anorexia?*
- *Does the media make it difficult for women to experience their personal qualities and uniqueness and, if so, how?*

- *What is it about our society's gender expectations that leaves women with a distorted sense of their bodies?*

We invited them to reflect on the expectations and roles of the women within their families through sharing photos and stories of female family members.

The results of these conversations initially proved surprising to us. The young women did not link their lives with our belief about the condition of women in our society. Contrary to ours, their experience was that 'women have come a long way'. They believed that in some families women had adopted dominant roles, making decisions and speaking up against the control of women.

Even when the media's portrayal of women in the fashion industry was discussed, the correlation between the manipulation of women and injustice appeared absent. Instead, when speaking of models such as Kate Moss, the participants seemed to express feelings of anger at the media hype associated with her appearance being described as 'anorexic'. They did not believe she was too thin and she definitely did not fit the picture of anorexia because she weighed more than them. One young woman almost left the group after this conversation, telling us privately later that she weighed the same as Kate Moss. She expressed feeling very depressed for, whilst Kate Moss was famous earning large appearance fees, she had been admitted to hospital.

Overall, the young women appeared initially to us to lack a political understanding of not only their experiences in relation to anorexia nervosa, but also of the experiences of women. On reflection however, we believe that it was we who were making an inappropriate assumption that the group would want to understand their experiences in terms of these discourses about women which we held to be true.

By the end of these sessions on gender we had done exactly what we had been fighting against throughout the program. We had attempted to impose our ideas and the meanings we had developed about gender and our society onto these young women, instead of more carefully exploring the participants' own experiences of gender and the meanings they associated with these experiences. We too hastily made the inaccurate assumption that as women our beliefs would be shared by other women. In bringing to the group ready-made political concepts, we perhaps thwarted the possibility of engaging the group in making their own analysis. The result was that the political context was explored by us in ways that appeared to have a limited relevance to the participants.

In contrast, as we explored the participants' views about the gender of the monster, we found that we began to engage in a more politically oriented discussion. The young women were able to be clear about how they viewed the differences between men and women in our society through this process. In that session they all identified the monster as male.

> ... [the monster is] *Male because he is rude, powerful and in control* ...

> ... *Male because he rules me* ... *men are always controlling* ... *it's like I'm a prisoner and he is the guard* ...

> ... *Male because he is so arrogant he has to be a guy* ...

> ... *It's like a male version of myself* ...

This last comment was elaborated by them saying :

> ... *As a male figure the monster is definitely not a wimp. It is domineering* ...

> ... *He is like everything you want to be but too extreme* ...

The group members thought that the male version of themselves would be:

> ... *Rude, arrogant, pig, allowed to do things that I can't, doesn't get told off, has more freedom, good at sport, controlling* ...

We asked them how significant gender is in the life of the monster.

> ... *I think the monster attacks women more than men because even if men have the same problems they show things differently; more aggressively* ... *If they're violent or abusive people respond by saying he is going through a rough patch, let him relax and he'll be okay. But if a women is aggressive it's a real big deal* ...

> ... *Girls always need to be seen as happy, in control and calm* ...

> ... *Society doesn't let me experience problems in the same way as men. For men it's cool to look big and strong but women need to look small, petite and skinny* ...

> ... *Men don't need to follow an image* ...

Opening up dialogue: the medical/psychiatric context .

In the second part of addressing the political context of the group, we invited the young women to examine the impact and experience of the medical and psychiatric treatment they had received. We were curious to know how the young people felt their 'disorder' was being understood by health professionals, and whether they felt that their individual treatment was based on model prescriptions rather than their own unique set of circumstances. It has been our experience that treatment regimes sometimes appear to blame the individual and as such generate interventions that can be controlling and even punitive. We wondered whether the young women felt they had any power to influence change in the processes allegedly designed to help them. These conversations revealed to us how powerless these young people felt in relation to the health systems.

They spoke of feeling invisible as individuals and resented being treated as if they were 'just another anorexic'.

... All people suffering from anorexia are not the same and shouldn't be treated as if they are ...

... Some people don't ask you what would be helpful. They make assumptions about that for you and don't acknowledge you. This makes you want to fight them more; makes you want to gain weight [to prove their assumptions wrong] *...*

Some spoke of feeling that at times the treating team would forget how hard it is to fight against the negativity monster and would become angry and frustrated forgetting that they also wanted the monster out of their lives.

... Some nurses and therapists act as if we are doing it [anorexia] *on purpose, because we chose to or because we want attention and control. It may begin that way but once you're into it the reasoning and control goes and all you want to do is make it stop ...*

... It feels like staff really don't understand what we are experiencing. They think we are playing games so they get frustrated with us and make decisions about our management. It felt like they were punishing us. They do this out of frustration but it's not fair that we have to cop their anger ...

They felt that the health system lacked respect for them, dismissing their points of view as insignificant.

> ... *It feels pointless giving your opinion when they ask what you would like to see on your management plan as they seldom agree and therefore don't include your ideas. It can feel patronising like they are playing a game with you when they ask you what you want and then ignore or worse ridicule what you say when they think you can't hear them* ...

Some treatment strategies were also seen by the group as unhelpful.

> ... *You feel bad about yourself as you put on weight* [through the Naso-Gastric tube] *without your control and so as soon as you leave the hospital all you want to do is lose the weight* ...

> ... *Instead* [of being helpful, forced bed-rest] *makes things worse as you realise things are so bad that fighting is too hard, so you give up* ...

> ... *Sitting at the same spot where you have just eaten makes you concentrate on what you have just eaten and this leads to you feeling less hopeful about change* ...

Interestingly to us, the young women were well aware of a tension within the dominant health system between two different approaches, one which sees anorexia nervosa primarily as a physical problem, and the other which sees it as a mental problem. The young people highlighted how ridiculous it felt to them that the treatment of the body and mind were being managed by two different services and felt that the psychiatric unit and the medical ward were working separately not as a partnership.

The young women were very open about their thoughts not only of what treatments they felt were not helpful, but also of possible changes that could be developed. Their comments highlighted that these young women felt neither understood nor respected by the systems that have been set up to assist them. Through this process, we became interested in the possibility of involving those with the power to address their concerns in listening to the group's ideas.

We explored with the group the idea of formulating a letter to be sent to the relevant professionals. The young women themselves, however, felt that a meeting with staff would be more effective and astonished us with their determination to make a difference. Consequently, a meeting was organised between the group and the head of nursing on the Medical Ward and the psychiatrist in charge of the Inpatient Unit. It became a vehicle for recruiting an audience to assist the young people with the development of new identities.

Recruiting an audience to preferred identities

The idea of recruiting an audience to bear witness to a person's changed identity stems from White's exploration of definitional ceremonies which he translated for use in reflective team processes (White 1995). Audiences act as an avenue whereby people's claims about their lives, including changed views about their histories and identities, can be witnessed. Once witnessed, these claims become acknowledged and authenticated, and thus more easily able to be incorporated into a person's new sense of self. It also provides a platform on which these preferred identities can receive affirming feedback assisting in cementing their existence. As mentioned earlier, group participants were already acting as witnesses to each other's evolving self-narratives.

The medical/psychiatric staff as an audience

We met with the head of nursing and the head of the adolescent psychiatric unit to help them understand the experiences of the group and the background to the proposed meeting. They both listened to our concerns, and appeared prepared to enter the meeting without preconceived ideas about the likely outcome.

At the meeting, the young women were able to share their concerns about the current system and its treatment of them, as well as express their views about different management strategies and change. The psychiatrist and nurse were initially invited to listen whilst the young women spoke, after which they were encouraged to give their comments and feedback. After this session, some of the young women stated that it felt like the first time that their views were listened to. Others believed it to be important as it provided the staff with a better understanding of their experiences of anorexia.

In speaking later to the psychiatrist about the session, he spoke of it as an invaluable exercise enabling him to gain a greater understanding of these young people's experiences, as well as an insight into the impact of certain medical and therapeutic practices. He acknowledged his surprise at the clarity, honesty and determination of the group members, and recognised that he too carried assumptions about 'anorexics'.

The outcome of this meeting was that formal meetings were established between the Inpatient Unit and the Medical Unit. (These had previously occurred on an *ad hoc* basis). In addition, when considering the implementation of new treatment models, the idea of inviting the young people to act as consultants was accepted as a useful strategy. An inaugural forum was held which included staff, the young women from the Busting Out - Breaking Free group, as well as others who had been in-patients in the past, to discuss practice ideas and share treatment options.

Through finding their voices and daring to confront and challenge those in power, the young women as a group had entered and influenced the political domain. They had also begun the process of not only seeing themselves in alternative ways, but being witnessed doing so.

The family as an audience

In addition to recruiting the hospital staff as an audience to preferred identities, we also felt that their families could act as important witnesses and supports to change. We wanted to meet with the parents of the young people as our experience had been that the significance of parents to the change process was often underestimated. We hoped to share with them the activities of the group and hear about their experiences. In particular, we wanted to hear their ideas about their daughters' situations, as well as gain some understanding of their views about anorexia and the treating systems. We put it to the members and they agreed.

Together we wondered how to do this. We could have a combined group with parents and the young women, or a separate group with the parents alone. In sharing the options with the group, the young women were adamantly in favour of the former, but also felt they would be threatened and uncomfortable in the same room as their parents. When the idea was suggested that we might try as an experiment a reflective process using the one-way screen (based on Andersen 1987), they jumped at the idea. This experiment seemed appealing to them not the least because the young people had, during their treatment, experienced the 'being observed part' of the one-way screen and resented it. They had never had the opportunity to be observers.

So, for part of the session, the group sat behind the screen observing their parents in discussion with one of the facilitators. The young people were, in most part, quiet throughout their parents' discussion, although were quick to remark when they felt their parents were embarrassing them by speaking of their strengths. Then, for the latter part of the session, they joined their parents to share some of their reflections.

Once the young people were in the same room as their parents they were uniformly and self-consciously silent. Perhaps the group was as yet not ready to have the changes they were making and their newly forming identities so openly discussed. Possibly the format of having all the parents together as witnesses was too threatening or confronting. It is difficult to know as no specific feedback about their experiences, other than they felt that it was a really positive experience, was obtained. Possibly, the feedback indicates that the group did not feel they needed to reflect in front of their parents in order to feel that the process had been helpful.

The parents shared with us the impact anorexia had had on their lives:

... I did feel a lot of guilt ... what have I done wrong ...

... affects us deeply ... suppress emotions...you become a boiling pot ...

... The monster has split our family in two, forcing people to take sides. I didn't think anything would be powerful enough to shake up our family ...

... The anorexia made us treat her differently to her brothers and sisters. It made us act in ways we never thought we would. Blackmail became common practice ...

In light of their comments, which at times appeared to us to suggest feelings of guilt and blame, we as a group talked about the parents' experiences of the treating systems. They acknowledged feeling at times that their attempts to assist their daughters were harshly judged by the health systems. Some spoke of feeling that their experiences had been minimised and that they were being blamed for anorexia's existence. This process of talking about their experience acted as a source of much-needed strength and support, and enabled some to question the assumptions being made about them and their family.

The second and final parent group met at the end of the program. In this session, parents openly shared with us their more recent understandings and experiences of both their own and their daughters' fight with the monster.

... I see it like a prison. They are hating themselves like a prisoner in a room with an invisible guard ... they attempt to get out everyday but they can't ...

... We've felt our daughter is less alone in the world by coming to the group ... gains confidence from sharing fears and wants ... not so defensive ... calmer ... more confident ...

... I initially thought she would just come out of it. I don't now ... whatever underlying problem causes anorexia I can see they are being controlled ... we are finding that it doesn't help to push, it just makes us feel depressed and angry ... backing off results in her expressing her feelings and making decisions for herself ... she's finding herself again. Our relationship with our daughter has improved. She is happier, more positive ... leaves me able to reclaim my own life back ...

From this and other feedback, our overall experience of the parent groups led us to the following conclusions:

1. Parents feel that they seldom have the opportunity to explore the impact of anorexia on their lives and hence on their relationships with their children and other family members.

2. Health professionals appear to promote ideas that result in parents feeling blamed for their daughter's difficulties which makes it hard for them to feel they can be a positive part of the change process.

3. The deep emotional impact of living with anorexia is minimised.

4. The role parents play as part of the change process, as well as witnesses to change, is under-valued.

5. Groups specifically for parents in which they are encouraged to share their own experiences can be extremely useful.

Reinforcing changed identities

In our view, one of the results of the political and social context surrounding anorexia is that young women often feel very negative about themselves. This is conceptualised as 'low self-esteem' by dominant psychological and psychiatric approaches which has the effect of locating the problem within the individual and making the context invisible. Such concepts of 'low self-esteem' then further reinforce young women's poor opinion of themselves because they reinforce the sense of individual responsibility for the problem.

It seemed to us that in their interactions with doctors, nurses and therapists, conversations about these young people were often problem-focussed, and were encouraging the young people to view themselves more and more as 'anorexics', rather than as people with an eating difficulty and a variety of other qualities such as a great sense of humour, ambitions in life, and a good ear for music. Therefore, as well as exploring the social and political context of anorexia and developing supportive audiences, we engaged the young women in a series of self-defined tasks, the purpose of which was to strengthen the young women's sense of personal agency and self-knowledge. We wanted these tasks to assist in the establishment of identities outside of the dominant story of ill-health and negativity.

Each participant was asked to consider a task that they could plan and complete by the end of the eleven sessions. The task was preferably to be something they had always wanted to do but had been unable to for whatever reason. The task itself did not need to be related to why they were in the group or their current difficulties.

All members completed a task (or two!) by the end of the eleven sessions. At the final session these tasks were displayed to the group and the group was invited to act as an audience giving feedback about the qualities these tasks highlighted for that individual.

One of the members created and decorated a 'Feeling Diary' which she felt could help her manage difficult emotions. She openly shared with the group her recent entry. The group's response to this task was that they felt it showed qualities including: insight into feelings, honesty, creativity, patience, perseverance, bravery, and a willingness to accept imperfections.

Attending a concert and decorating a box as a Christmas gift were other tasks completed. The concert was something that this young woman had wanted to attend but doubted being able to due to her ill-health. She spoke about being able to achieve this by sticking to her meal plan and keeping out of hospital. The qualities the group highlighted in this instance were: determination, strength, motivation, imagination, and fortitude.

Conclusion

The feedback from the young women and their parents at the end of the group gives a clear sense of the outcomes they experienced from participating in the group. It is important to note that these outcomes were not expressed in relation to eating or not eating. Indeed, they were more commonly bound by a sense of hope that did not appear present in the group at its onset.

From the young people themselves:

... I have become less self-conscious ... I talk more openly and can say what I feel without feeling ashamed ...

... I am going quite well as I managed to stay out of hospital for longer than I ever have. I'd rather try to stay out and have fun; have some sort of life instead of sitting in hospital all the time ...

... I began to feel a bit more hopeful and a bit less depressed - I was glad to talk with people with similar difficulties and experiences ...

... I feel as if I am beating the 'negativity monster' and facing my real problems now. I feel better knowing there are people sharing my problems and that there is a group which really helps me ...

... My positive attitude would probably stand out the most. My confidence and social interactions would also be something noticeably different. Also the fact that I now want and make my voice heard, whereas before I could never do that ...

And from the parents:

... She's more interested in getting on with others and socialising ...

... The group broke down a lot of barriers. She is now able to speak more

freely ...

... My daughter seemed to feel more important ... it helped her understand and respect everyone's feelings in the family ... [I feel she became less] *afraid of anorexia ...*

... Enthusiasm was the first [change], *and then we noticed that she had thought about her feelings more and was able to put into words what she felt. Also her confidence increased. She felt it was okay to feel how she felt and not have to hide it ...*

... I am a lot more relaxed about my daughter's situation. I know there is always someone to talk to. My daughter is also a lot more communicative ...

The words of one young woman who took part in the group caught our attention and continues to hold it:

... After unmasking the devil which has plagued my life for what seems like forever, and the many tricks he has played on me, I can confidently say that I shall never fall back into the routine of taking laxatives after eating, no matter how much pressure the devil places upon me. Hopefully I am on the road to 'busting out-breaking free' of the devil's grasp. I know it will be a long and hard struggle and that there may be some steps in the backward direction, but I truly believe that once the devil is unmasked and his trickery revealed, only then can you say that a life with anorexia nervosa is no life at all - rather it is a glimpse of hell ...

This vividly portrays to us the desperation experienced by young women who are trying to rid themselves of anorexia. These words challenge us to consider how we, as treating professionals, have been supportive of her devil's influence. Through our experience in the group we found that, allowed a voice, these young women were more than capable of making a significant contribution to reviewing aspects of the intervention process. The process also emphasised to us that there is strength in numbers when you are fighting such a powerful opponent. The outcomes of the program illustrated that young women diagnosed with anorexia can benefit from working together in a group. Most importantly, however, we need to recognise that the fight against the monster that is anorexia nervosa begins with our recognition of just how easy it is for us, as health professionals, to succumb to those practices which promote self-doubt and self-criticism. This young woman's demon is our own in another form. For us, as workers, the group process was also an effective way of bringing these issues into focus so that we could start to find ways of addressing them.

Acknowledgements

Firstly we would like to acknowledge the young women who took the time to share with us the stories of their lives and the risk to begin re-authoring their lives. Without these women this paper would not have been possible. Our lives have been enriched by each and every one of them.

Secondly we would like to thank the Child and Adolescent Psychiatry Department at Monash Medical Centre for giving us the space to run the group. In particular we thank the staff of both the medical and psychiatric wards who gave their time to the group. Their support and interest in both the narrative approach and our questioning of the system was invaluable.

Finally, we give our appreciation to both Tony Silver and Joe Tucci. Firstly to Tony for providing us with colour and humour. We thank him for his lasting support. Secondly to Joe whose continuous encouragement, care and guidance gave birth to a multiplicity of possibilities. We are thankful for his enthusiasm in the process and his ability to instil in us a motivation to take risks.

Notes

1. First published in Vol.3 of the 1997 *Gecko*. Republished here with permission.

2. It was thanks to adolescent psychiatry that Kate and Marilyn met and connected. It was thanks to the young people who were in the grip of anorexia that Marilyn and Kate were able to understand how, inadvertently, psychiatric knowledges and practices were tightening anorexia's grip. And it was thanks to narrative ideas that Kate and Marilyn were able to learn from the same young people about important grip-loosening, anti-anorexic tactics.

   Marilyn continues to learn from the people who consult her and has found ways of sharing some of these learnings with others. She can be contacted at the Reflections Consultancy, Training and Counselling Service, PO Box 4035, Ringwood, Victoria 3134, Australia, phone (03) 9421 0882.

   Kate currently enjoys 'turning poison into medicine' while discovering anti-problem ways in and around families. She can be contacted at the Canterbury Family Centre in Melbourne, Victoria, Australia, phone (03) 9882 8336.

References

Andersen, T. 1987: 'The reflecting team: Dialogue and meta-dialogue in clinical work.' *Family Process*, 26:415-428.

Epston, D. 1993: 'Internalizing discourses versus externalizing discourses.' In Gilligan, S. & Price, R. (eds), *Therapeutic Conversations*, pp.161-177. New York: W.W.Norton & Co.

Epston, D. & White, M. 1992: 'Consulting your consultants: The documentation of alternative knowledges.' In Epston, D. & White, M.: *Experience, Contradiction, Narrative and Imagination: Selected Papers of David Epston and Michael White*, pp.11-26. Adelaide: Dulwich Centre Publications.

Estes, C.P. 1992: *Women who Run with the Wolves*. London: Rider.

Ghostbusters. Produced by Columbia Pictures, 1984.

MacSween, M. 1993: *Anorexic Bodies: A Feminist and Sociological Perspective on Anorexia Nervosa*. London: Routledge.

Tanzer, K. 1997: 'When the "I" means "we".' *Gecko*, 2:65-77.

White, M. 1995: 'The politics of therapy.' In White, M., *Re-Authoring Lives: Interviews and Essays*, pp.41-59. Adelaide: Dulwich Centre Publications.

White, M. 1991: 'Deconstruction and therapy.' *Dulwich Centre Newsletter*, 3:21-40.

White, M. 1989: 'The externalizing of the problem and the re-authoring of lives and relationships.' In White, M., *Selected Papers*, pp.5-28. Adelaide: Dulwich Centre Publications.

White, M. & Epston, D. 1989: *Literate Means to Therapeutic Ends*. Adelaide: Dulwich Centre Publications. (Also published as White, M. & Epston, D. 1990: *Narrative Means to Therapeutic Ends*. New York: Norton.)

7

The Journey:
A narrative approach
to adventure-based therapy[1]

by[2]

Aileen Cheshire & Dorothea Lewis

In this paper we explore our experiences of travelling with students on a journey that is both physical and metaphorical. This journey involves ten days of vigorous and demanding cycling, tramping and sea kayaking. As counsellors, we work with the young people before and after The Journey as well as visiting them in the middle of the expedition. The Journey is an attempt to offer young people, who may well not be attracted to sitting talking in a counsellor's office, the opportunity to experience a sense of group belonging, the feeling of success, and the beauty of the outdoor environment. Most importantly, it is an attempt to offer young people the chance to experience themselves in new and exciting ways and to build upon stories about themselves that will enrich their lives over time.

Authors' dilemmas

In the process of writing up our work we have faced a number of dilemmas. We have wondered how to do justice to the richness of the experience of our work with young people. We have also struggled with the political implications of representing other people's experiences on paper. This seems a particularly important issue when we as adults and workers are attempting to describe the experiences of the young people with whom we work, and when these young people prefer not to be named in the text. How can we give space to the voices of young people while ensuring that we are not appropriating their experiences? We are grateful to David Denborough for helping us to find a way of writing that allows these dilemmas to be recognised and faced.

It seems that in the process of writing we encounter similar dilemmas to those that we face in our daily work. How can we as adults find ways of working and writing that question what it means to be an adult and a professional and that open possibilities for collaboration with young people?

Context

We both work as counsellors at Selwyn College, which is a large co-educational multi-cultural school in East Auckland. Nearly half the students have English as a second language and there are 46 different first languages in the school. Because of its broad senior curriculum and its distinctive liberal philosophy, it attracts a wide range of students from all over Auckland.

We see our role as counsellors as being to help students co-author alternative stories to previously dominant problem-saturated stories about themselves and their lives (see White & Epston 1990). We look for competence and solutions rather than focusing on inadequacies. We try to take a counselling stance of attentiveness and respectful curiosity about students' lives, accompanied by a belief that the students are the experts on their own lives. Having genuine dialogue with students means abandoning the notion of counsellor as expert with a privileged view and instead becoming a partner in the generation of new, preferred ways of living.

We have learnt, in our one-to-one counselling work with students, that opening space for the building of preferred stories is not always easy, especially for young people who often have limited agency in their lives. Experiences which enable students to have a different contextual relationship with the problems dominating their lives can be few and far between. We believe that outdoor experiences can provide a context which can enable students to develop different relationships with the problems in their lives. We believe that The Journey is a means of opening space for new stories.

We are both people who delight in spending time away from the city. I (Dorothea) am someone who spends most of her holidays tramping, sea kayaking and having outdoor adventures with groups of friends. I know personally of the excitement of achieving expedition goals, the pleasures of being away from city pressures, and the closeness of living with a group of others away from the rest of the world. I know of the sense of self-confidence and harmony that I always seem to have when returning from a trip away.

Similarly I (Aileen) have a long history of longing to 'get away' into the outdoors. I spent part of my childhood growing up on a farm. Riding my horse gave me an enormous sense of freedom and an experience of myself that was quite different from my experiences of myself at boarding school. There was nothing like coming home from school in the holidays and being free to roam.

From our own lives we know of the power of outdoor experiences. We have also, over the years, witnessed students who have struggled at school in a myriad of different ways find alternative ways of being when they are away from school. We have learnt that while for some students the experience itself is enough for them to understand their lives and themselves differently, for others, making meaning of the experience in collaborative conversations is useful. We have been exploring ways of making the most of the experiences that the young people have while on the expedition. We believe that so much more can be achieved than just allowing the experience to happen and having everyone say how wonderful it had been for them.

Counselling is one thread or strand of the program, interwoven with the two other strands of group work and physical challenge. It is the binding together of all three that gives The Journey its strength. The group work provides the atmosphere of the program and an audience for change, the physical challenge provides the context and catalyst, and individual counselling provides a way of making meaning of the experience. The combination of these strands provides the possibility for translating new experiences during the expedition into longer term changes in relation to the ways in which students understand themselves and their lives.

The beginning

In order to open the program up to all students who might be interested we advertise it through many different forums in the school. These include speaking to assemblies, notices around the school, Deans, Counsellors, Form Teachers directly inviting individuals, the Management Team speaking to parents and students they are involved with, and newsletters that are sent to students' homes. Anyone between the ages of 15 and 18 has the opportunity to apply for a place.

Once we have advertised we believe that it is important for us to leave it up to individual students to show their interest and apply. In our programs, we work from the standpoint of offering information and support and then standing back to allow young people to make decisions. Our interest is in encouraging self-referral, self-responsibility ,and for the student to be in control of their choices.

This means that some students in the school who are causing concern will decide that this program does not appeal to them. It also means that we are acting consistently with the belief that young people have the capacity to make good decisions about their lives. In this way every step becomes a possibility for learning and for the students to take control of their lives.

Entry into the program

Application forms, a pamphlet, and an explanatory letter to parents are made available from the Counselling receptionist, and students who are interested pick them up from there. The application takes the form of a parents' permission letter and medical form. A completed, signed form, returned to the receptionist, is the completion of the first step into the program. At times we have had more than forty applications for ten places, and the numbers seem to be growing as the program becomes more known each year.

A good deal of discussion takes place at this stage as parents and students ask for more details and explore whether or not the program is suitable for them. Students are invited to reflect on their reasons for applying, to consider the following questions and to write down their responses.

- *Please tell us about what attracts you to apply for The Journey.*
- *What qualities do you have that might help you succeed on The Journey?*
- *Which of these qualities, if any, would you like to develop more?*
- *What things would you like to be different when The Journey is finished?*

Considering these questions, and writing down the responses, is often an opportunity for students to begin to articulate alternative stories about themselves, stories that focus on strengths, competencies and resources. It is hoped that these stories will develop throughout the program. We believe that the therapeutic work begins when the application forms are first asked for. It is hoped that the conversations during the time of selection can create a context for students to begin to learn about themselves in new ways. The seeds of alternative stories are sown before the program begins.

Selection interviews

Selection interviews are the next step in building a counselling relationship. These interviews also offer the possibility of setting the atmosphere of self-reflection and respectful conversation. We feel it is important that students know that this is an integral part of the program before they make a full commitment to it. Our questions explore goals, expectations of change, hopes and histories, and we are clear about our underlying belief that the program offers the possibilities of meaningful change. Our questions are similar to those on the written applications but in conversation explorations of greater depth become possible.

Last year, Andrew[3] was one of the keenest students in enquiring about the program. He had developed an 'A+ bad reputation' in his two years at Selwyn. When 'trouble' loomed large in his school life he had come to both of us for support. Unfortunately, however, despite all attempts to challenge his 'on-the-edge lifestyle', nothing had been able to assist him to escape from the strong clutches of 'trouble'. Andrew's opening statement in response to our wondering about his enthusiasm for the program was: *Something has to change. I've got to do something, because nothing's worked so far. And things are pretty bad.*

Many students, like Andrew, see the program as a last chance. Many young people's lives are constrained by broader contexts and stories in ways that make interacting with the structures of schooling very difficult. The Journey is seen to offer the possibility of a different context. When we spoke with Andrew about the impact that an 'on-the-edge lifestyle' was having on Andrew's life and what sort of future he thought this was leading too, he had no doubts that expulsion from school and trouble with the police would be part of that sort of future. For young men in Andrew's position, the opportunity for new ways of relating are often yearned for, as the following transcript of our conversation describes:

What is it about The Journey that has led you to hope that this could be a way of having a different future?

I've done Cubs and Scouts and things like that, and I know what that does for you. Getting away from everything and having a chance to think about things ... It might be a chance for me to feel better about myself.

Do you have any ideas about the things in yourself that you would like to feel better about?

Well my Dad keeps saying that one day soon he'll see me brought home in a box, he thinks it is so bad ... and I'd like to show him I can do something.

What would that do for your ideas about yourself Andrew?

I'd like my parents to be able to believe in me.

Would that be like building a bridge to them?

Yeah.

How would you feel about yourself then?

Much stronger ... it would take the hassles out of things ...

Building on changes

For other students the program is seen as a chance to build upon and strengthen changes that they have already made. Last year this was true for the majority of the group. Young people often find ingenious ways of making a path for their lives. For some, The Journey represents another step along the way. Neomai commented that in fourth form last year she had a really bad year, *'wagging lots of classes'*, *'not interested in school'*, *'in lots of trouble'*. Fifth form had been going much better for her with the structured support and clear goals of the Basketball Academy. She had learnt that *discipline really helps*. She said that she would not have thought of applying for The Journey a year ago, and the fact that she was interested now was due in part to her new-found belief in herself that she could do things. Building on these new-found strengths was her main aim.

Having students who are building on changes they have already made alongside students who have a sense of urgency about the need to start to make changes, allows the possibility for young people to learn from each other. The issues that young people face are often seen as individual problems. Learning collectively provides the opportunity to place responsibility for problems back where it belongs - with the broader structures and practices of the culture.

The diversity of young people involved also sets The Journey somewhat apart from other programs designed solely for 'at-risk' young people. Students have illustrated to us the power of language and labels when they have asked, 'This isn't just for kids with big problems, is it?' With students coming together from different places and experiences, the possibilities for students to learn from each other are endless. Learning is never a one-way process - there are usually new learnings in all the relationships within the group. For us, as counsellors, this is also true. Feeling a part of a team that is working on problems and dilemmas, rather than as isolated individuals, brings sustenance and energy to our work and personal lives.

Meeting the families

We try, where possible and appropriate, to involve the families of students in the life of the program. We invite family members to participate in creating the climate in which change is possible. Each family is contacted by phone and, where appropriate, is invited to meet with us individually one evening at school. This is a good time for passing on information and answering questions about the program.

In one family interview I (Aileen) began by asking Timoti questions about his hopes for the program. As he explained his goal of building better relationships with his family, I was aware his mother was listening very attentively. When I asked her whether what he was saying was what she expected or whether there was some element of surprise, she responded by explaining that he had never taken the initiative to do something like this before: *Getting himself organised to do this is an absolutely new thing.* We then went on to talk about what it might mean if he was able to build on this achievement. The conversation offered Timoti and his mother a different experience of each other. To witness a young man speak of wanting to honour and build upon his relationship with family, and for this to lead to a new connectedness between mother and son, seems to illustrate the power for change that can occur when different contexts are created for conversations.

Ben, on the other hand, talked about his goals of learning to work co-operatively with others. I (Aileen) asked his aunt if these goals were what she would have expected or whether there were some surprises and she replied: *I'm absolutely blown away by what he wants to do. I think these are wonderful.* The main focus of this session was highlighting the particular qualities of Ben that his aunt believed might be useful for him in the program. Ben's pleasure in hearing the descriptions of his strengths was obvious from his grin and his own contributions. He explained that he had *been through a fair bit,* but that now things were going more the way he wanted and this was what he wanted to build on. Watching caring conversations like this one, between young men and older women in their lives, offers me considerable hope.

With some families the story of 'trouble' is so dominant that the sense of hope is very small. Stephen's mother thought, *He might as well give it a go, but it doesn't have much chance of working.* When further questions were asked (by Dorothea) possibilities became clearer:

Do you think there might be a difference with this, in that Stephen has pursued it himself?

Stephen's mother: *Yeah, well maybe, but he doesn't last at anything.*

How do you feel when you hear your Mum say that?

Stephen: *Yeah, it's true.*

Do you think there is anything different about The Journey that might mean that you could see it through? Do you think there is any hope for The Journey and you?

Stephen: *Mmm. Yeah. I chose it.*

Stephen's mother: *Yes, that's true. So far I've chosen everything. Like taking him to counselling, and he only will come for one session. Maybe if he really wants this it might help more.*

Young people often have so little power over their own lives in our culture that being able to choose to go on The Journey can become highly significant. In conversations in which hope is hard to find, we have experienced that keeping the focus on noticing very small changes has been helpful. The experience of being able to choose is one that can often be built upon.

Our main hope of involving family members in the program is to enlist their support for the young person and to provide an audience who can imagine and witness changes that may occur. Family members often have information that can be useful in identifying possible stumbling blocks and they often hold an appreciation of the history of the young people's strengths. With the restraints on young people's lives in our culture so strong, this broader audience is often invaluable.

The group program

After the interviews with the young people and family members, the final selections for The Journey are made and group work begins. Before the expedition, three sessions of group work are held, but first a two day 'Adventure training workshop' takes place.

The Challenge Ropes Course[4]

The group meet each other for the first time when they are picked up at school by a taxivan that delivers them to the Challenge Ropes Course at Henderson High School. We deliberately choose to start the program in this way because the Challenge Ropes Course over two days lays the foundation for how the group will operate. In adventure-based learning terminology this is know as 'setting the bedrock'. It involves initiative exercises, group problem-solving, personal goal-setting, and developing group commitments to each other and the process. The young people have often commented on the noticeable differences between the group on the first morning when everyone is feeling shy and slightly uncomfortable, and the group on the second day when there is generally a feeling of cohesion.

Group sessions at school

Between the Challenge Ropes Course and the beginning of The Journey we hold three group sessions with the aim of building on the strengths of the group and developing an atmosphere of trust and respect.

Session One

Last year our first group session began with us all watching an edited twenty-minute video of activities on the ropes course as a means of bringing us up-to-date with group developments. The group was intrigued and excited and we found ourselves joining the excitement and missing some opportunities for constructive conversations. On reflection we could have made much more of this video by asking questions such as:

- *What things do you notice about the way the group is working?*
- *Are there any things that are different between activities early in the program and those at the end?*
- *If so, what do those things tell you about the group?*
- *Are there things you notice about yourself that are different between*

activities early in the program and those at the end?

- *If so what do you think of these differences? What do you think enabled you to do things in a different way?*

Our focus in this session is to build on what had been done on the ropes course to develop the group. We ask the students to choose any number of words from Project Adventure 'feeling cards' that are scattered on the floor to describe their experience of the group in the two days of the ropes course. The cards are put on the floor in front of each student as they explain their experiences. Words which describe the qualities of the group are then brainstormed onto the whiteboard and a distinction is made between qualities the group wants to retain and those they think need changing. How those changes might be achieved is also discussed.

Session Two

This session is designed to encourage more personal reflection and talking. Students individually work on personal shields, using words, pictures, symbols, or whatever they choose. The four sections of the shield are:

- personal qualities that support you;
- experiences or events in your life that have been important;
- values, beliefs, ideas that are important to you;
- hopes and dreams for the future.

Across the bottom, a motto or phrase of how the students would like others to think of them is included.

Last year the group took this task seriously and worked quietly for an hour or more. They then each showed their work to the group, and had the option of choosing which bits they would speak about. An atmosphere of deepening trust and confidence in each other was gradually developed. The session ended with a discussion on the group contract. All ideas were brainstormed and then discussed. It was decided that a printed version of the contract would be produced in between sessions, ready for a group signing in the next session.

Session Three

This is the last session before the group leaves on the expedition. We try to plan this session in a way that caters for all the differing needs within the group. Last year the session began with students in pairs talking and questioning each other on their hopes for The Journey and how they saw The Journey impacting on their future lives. Each student then chose an object or objects to symbolise or represent their hopes from a pile we had assembled. The group sat at one end of the room as each student placed their object at the other end and spoke to the group about what it represented. The exercise seems to allow for the expression of young people's creativity and originality.

Hannah described a children's three-dimensional puzzle as representing the choices, risks and experiments she was making. She was, she said, *trying to figure things out*. The black rock she held represented her wish to be someone of depth, someone of value. Ben held a complex origami construction, explaining that the torn bit showed his life as it was *a while ago - a bit messed up*, but that the points of the construction showed all the possibilities he was now seeing.

Pairs were formed again and, this time, possible obstacles to their hopes were discussed. Regathering at the end of the room, we used large cushions to represent the obstacles. Each student placed as many cushions as they wished across the middle of the room and talked about the things they saw as obstacles. Many had a shared theme. Self-doubt and difficulties in resisting the invitations of friends to get side-tracked were common. Young people often face restraints from youth culture, families and the broader adult world that can restrict their vision and distort their views of themselves. This situation was metaphorically represented within the group session by the fact that the objects of hope were eventually completely blocked from view by the wall of cushions.

Finally, the group explored what they had as a group that would enable them to break through the obstacles and we wrote these on sheets of paper in front of them. Then, standing on these sheets of paper and yelling things like *go for it!*, they leapt on the wall of cushions, flattening them. Trying to find ways of acting collectively to break through barriers in all of our lives is an invigorating process. This was a session with a great deal of energy and laughter.

The group was then introduced to Tania and Mark, from Adventure Specialists Trust, who were to lead them on the expedition, and together they discussed the practical aspects of the trip. Anticipation was strong and there was a definite air of excitement.

The Journey

The expedition phase of The Journey is run by a specialist firm called Adventure Specialists Trust. We have full confidence in the care that they take and in their personal work with the students. Their ways of processing experiences, debriefing activities, and questioning to deepen understanding and experience, fit very comfortably with our ways of working. They organise and guide the young people through the ten-day expedition.

In 1996, the route of The Journey involved travelling from Waitangi back to Selwyn College in Auckland. Once the group reach their starting point by minibus, the students do the full distance back 'under their own steam'. This involves cycling, tramping and sea kayaking over 400 kilometres. Each of the ten days of The Journey has a separate theme. It is introduced after breakfast, usually with a story or reading, and is continued throughout the day, ending with a group discussion each evening. Some of the themes include 'a temporary community', 'a new beginning', 'life values', 'risks', 'perseverance', 'where are you heading?', 'life is a challenge - meet it'. Each day has a leader from the group, and at the end of the day the leader is given feedback about the way the day has gone.

The physical demands of this adventure are extreme, particularly as most of the students are not especially fit. The first day is a 96 kilometre bike ride, for example. All of the students find themselves pushed to the limit physically over the ten days. Mental attitude becomes the issue. Things which were previously seen as personal problems begin to be seen in the context of what the students are learning physically. Not giving up; discovering that your limits are different to what you thought, helping others, facing difficulties as a group, and being positive, are some of the lessons that the young people have articulated as important. As The Journey progresses, the students start to experience their own strength and often begin to see the problems they left behind in Auckland in a different light.

The counselling aspect of the expedition phase

We have tried various different ways of structuring the counselling work during The Journey. We now prefer the model of the 'visiting counsellor'. Half-way through the expedition we arrive for an evening, bearing chocolate cake and news from home, and have an individual counselling session with each of the group members. This is then followed by a group session. The students know about this from the beginning and this year we found that many had been thinking throughout The Journey about what they wanted to 'notice' in their counselling session. Our intention is clear. We are continuing the process of co-constructing alternative or preferred stories that by this stage have already been identified. By doing this during The Journey itself there is the opportunity to 'seize the moment' and 'thicken' the preferred story. This is a vital stage in the process as it not only takes advantage of the situation but also enables the student to focus on the time remaining and the possibilities this provides.

It is not hard to be curious in these individual sessions. We find excitement catching. Our purpose is to explore what students have been experiencing, noticing and thinking. Articulating the details helps 'thicken' their preferred stories, so questions not only explore their own thoughts, feeling and actions, but also look at other perspectives. At the risk of taking questions out of context and therefore losing their tone and texture, we've listed some of the questions that we often ask:

- *Have things been as expected or have there been some surprises?*
- *Have there been things that you've done that at first you didn't think you'd be able to do?*
- *What was it that enabled you to do that?*
- *Now that you know this about yourself what difference does this make?*
- *Who would be least surprised at you doing that?*
- *What do you think that person would say to you now?*
- *Are there some things about this way of thinking or behaving that you want to strengthen or develop?*

Individual conversations

We both have clear memories of a special evening on our last journey. We had driven to meet the group at Dargaville, 150 kilometres north of Auckland. Early in the evening we each met with five students for individual conversations. In those conversations, Ken spoke about the ways in which he had been learning that he could get along very well with people from different backgrounds to him. His fears of being isolated could be looked at in a different light now that he had discovered that he had an ease with other people. What he had framed as a problem didn't seem like one at all now. He had also learned that powering ahead on his own mission to test his physical strength was not helpful to others in the group, and that his challenge was how to meet his own needs while leaving room for others. Witnessing a young man discover the ways in which being a part of a team was liberating seemed powerfully hopeful.

For Andrew, the discovery lay in his ability to support and encourage others. His challenge lay not so much in the physical tasks, but in being part of the group. Part of his dominant school story was how anger and impatience turned him against others who he saw as being *unfair* or *stupid*. Now, although frustrated and angered by the power of self-doubt and its influence on Hannah, Andrew had *put anger in the back seat* and got alongside Hannah, encouraging her and drawing her back into the group. His grin as he described his actions said it all - here was a sense of pride in discovering this different way of relating and therefore building a different sort of reputation within the group. To see a young woman and a young man working together in ways that challenged broader cultural stories and enriched both of their lives offered everyone a sense of collective pride and encouragement.

Rachel's story also offered us sustenance. Before The Journey, Rachel described it as: *my last chance to sort out my life.* She had been increasingly absent from school and had 'taken off' from home several times. When I (Aileen) began to talk with Rachel, she described the first few days of The Journey like this: *This is the very first time I haven't given up on myself. I'm helping myself for the very first time. I've always given up on myself before and now I know that, although I felt like giving up this time, I didn't.* It was a moment that seemed almost super-charged. Rachel went on to talk about what this had meant for her and in particular the thinking that she had been doing about her relationship with her mother. What Rachel was now realising was that her mother had never given up on her no matter what she had done or how she had behaved.

We recalled the conversation that Rachel, her mother and I had shared before The Journey began. Back then, Rachel's mother had spoken strongly about the qualities that she felt were special in Rachel - in particular her *awhi* (ability to love and care for others). Rachel said that at the time she hadn't really listened to her mother but now she was remembering her words. She was already excited about seeing her mother again and could well imagine what her mother might think and say about not giving up on herself.

Rachel did go home and rebuild a different sort of relationship with her mother. It was a relationship that provided strength and solidness for both of them when, two months after The Journey, Rachel, for a short time, heard voices and saw things that no-one else saw.

The young people shared with us, in our individual conversations, stories of how they had carved out new ways of relating while on the first half of The Journey. These stories laid the foundations for powerful group discussions.

The group conversation

By the time we had finished the individual conversations it was dark and raining. The dinner group had learned the hard way how long it takes to cook potatoes, and the whole evening had got later and later. It was ten o'clock when we were ready to start. With the rain tumbling down outside, our circle around a table in the middle of a large, shabby community hall seemed very intimate. The discoveries of the earlier individual conversations seemed to still be tangible as we sat down to talk.

Our hope for the evening was to increase the visibility of the changes which were appearing and to strengthen the support for those changes. We asked the group to speak to each member in turn, going around the circle, commenting on three areas:

1. *What have you have grown to appreciate about ... ?*
2. *Were there any surprises for you when you really got to know ... ?*

3. *What is a challenge you could set ... for the rest of The Journey?*

The students, whom teachers would regularly complain about in relation to their lack of focus and concentration, chose their words very deliberately and with an intense sense of caring. During the 90-minute session no-one made a joke about the process. There seemed to be a very real sense of responsibility towards what they were saying to each other. They were half-way through The Journey and the sense of community was strong. This session added further to this sense of community by enabling students to say to each other things that are often left unsaid. At the same time, this meant that the new stories that the young people were developing about themselves had a broader audience and could be supported and built upon. Each student heard other young people reflect publicly on the very things that they had been noticing about themselves and had talked about in their individual conversations earlier that evening. As students heard what others had to say about them, their reactions, which ranged from surprise to tears, spoke of the value of providing a respectful audience of peers.

Hannah had been struggling against negativity each day so far. She heard that others appreciated her sense of humour and her facility with words. Everyone in the group spoke of how surprised they were to find that she put herself down so much and brought herself low with negative thoughts when she had so much going for her. They set goals around turning negative thoughts into positives and offered to help with this. To witness the other young people find ways of collectively assisting Hannah to stand up to the restraints in her life as a young woman seemed to offer powerful examples to us in the adult world.

Some found what the others had to say very moving. Rachel sat with tears pouring down her face as she heard what others appreciated in her. Ken heard that others were surprised to find that he wasn't really like the person he made out to be at school, putting others down, being arrogant, but rather that he had been caring and really helpful to people who were struggling. His challenge was to be able to continue being such an open person towards others. To watch a young man step into different ways of being, outside of dominant masculine ways, while on The Journey, and to hear other young people speak openly of their experiences of this, was powerfully moving.

Arriving home

Ten days after setting out, the students kayaked into Kohimaramara, to find their parents waiting on the beach. It was an emotional moment. There was a flurry of excitement, hugging and tears, as they set off to walk the final 2 kilometres of The Journey up the hill to school where there was a formal *powhiri*[5] to welcome them back. This was held at lunchtime so that friends could be there too. The principals spoke, as did each of the students once the formal part was over. Then a lunch for everyone followed. The school clearly recognises that to do The Journey takes courage, strength and determination. The students left the ceremony feeling affirmed and proud of themselves.

Back to School

The first couple of weeks following the group's return are vital for cementing the new resolves and wishes to make things different back in Auckland. When we first began our involvement in The Journey, we did not know how to make the most of the experiences of the young people involved. If there is no ongoing support and strengthening of new stories they can quickly fall away when the invitations to former habits assert themselves. One young woman on our first program told us that she felt the best she had ever felt while she was away, but now that the group had been back awhile, she felt she had lost that feeling. As we talked, she helped us to realise the importance of incorporating the 'making meaning' part of the program and ensuring that it continues once back in school.

Straight after The Journey is a busy time with a lot of school-work to be caught up. We speak to teachers about realistic expectations and support for the students, particularly in noticing and reinforcing changes. It is also a busy time in the program with group meetings, individual counselling sessions, family meetings and a finale of two further days on the ropes course.

Our intentions are clear in these activities: we want to provide a context that will allow the strengthening of the preferred alternative stories that have been developed in all three strands of the program. This takes different forms. The audience for change continues to be the group itself as the bond they have developed builds over time. Further meetings with families widen the audience.

In our individual meetings, some of our questions focus on who is noticing and appreciating the steps that the students are taking. Even where the audience is limited, there is the possibility of exploring who they have known in the past who would appreciate these new developments.

Having permanent reminders creates resources which are always accessible. Students are given a certificate at the completion of The Journey as well as a folder containing the stories and readings used in the program. Any writing they have done is included. Later they also create a large photographic montage which is copied and laminated for each of them. The changes that students have made in relation to the ways in which they understand themselves and their lives are further supported by letters. We write each student a letter summarising the meetings we have had with them. These reminders are important, as students who have done The Journey in previous years have sometimes come back to school and told us that it was only after considerable time that they realised the true impact of The Journey in their lives. As they face new experiences in adult life and develop new stories, they can make different meaning of their experiences on The Journey.

Returning

Sometimes it is upon return to the school that the value of The Journey becomes most clear. I (Dorothea) remember a young man who did The Journey three years ago. He wanted to gain some self-confidence and work out where he was going in his life. He was then 16 and was experiencing severe 'teasing' at school. He was very quiet in the classroom, if not silent. His teachers felt they had never got to know him and he did not appear to have any close friends.

The day the group got back we had the usual *powhiri* with family and friends in the hall. His mum was there but no friends. I was moved when he stood up and told the assembled group how important the time away had been for him. He pointed out that he had never spoken up in a group before and for him to be standing up there and saying something about himself was 'awesome'. He had learned, he said, to speak out and to think of what he had to say as being worthwhile (before he never spoke out for fear of ridicule and being seen as 'useless'). He said that the feeling of belonging to the group had helped him to realise this, and that the things that the others had said to him while they had been away had made him feel accepted amongst his peers for the first time in his life.

After everyone had gone home that afternoon, I was approached by a teacher in the staffroom. She had been teaching biology when suddenly this young man, who would usually be in her class had he not been in the ceremony, came into the room. He said to the whole class, who had fallen silent when he came in the door, 'I've been on the most fantastic journey. Do you want me to tell you about it?' She was struck by the difference in his being as he walked in. She said it was as if he was standing tall. The class was eager and started asking questions, so she abandoned biology for the period and off he went. She said at first it was like a travelogue as he described the physical part of the adventure, but the remarkable thing to her was the silence in the room as his classmates listened with growing respect. They started to ask questions which led him into talking about what he had learned about living with a group, and how come he was standing there talking to them like this when he had never spoken in the class before. It was a powerful experience for both the teacher and the students in the class. It was a powerful experience for me to hear about it too. It is hard for me to imagine the courage it needed for him to walk into that classroom and face the very culture that had resulted in the put-downs and insults towards him. He taught me something about summoning courage. I try to remember his story whenever I need to take action in difficult circumstances.

Our experiences

This work is richly sustaining. It gives me (Dorothea) encouragement and sustains my belief in the ability of people to take control over the direction of their lives. It challenges me to work with others to create contexts where this can occur. From the young people in the program I have learnt about not giving up when the going is tough. I have learnt that I can go further than I first think. I have learned about the power of accepting support from others; about the possibility of risking trusting others even when you do not know them very well; and probably most of all about having the 'guts' to take the risk to explore a different way of being with people.

Personally, through my involvement in The Journey, I (Aileen) have done a great deal of thinking about how I have faced challenges in my own life and what has supported me in facing those challenges. In remembering some of these events I have been able to see more clearly what I drew on. That has come out of conversations with students where there seems to be little in the way of support or resources for their preferred ideas about themselves. I have learnt that there is always something or someone and that has got me thinking about past events in my own life.

In my work, the biggest change is that I have become much more attuned to what or who supports resilience, and I am more thorough in my attempts to make it possible to bring this history of support out into the open. I have heard this process described as 'small' work in the sense that often it is very small events, or someone a long time ago, who supported the resilience. I prefer to use the word 'fine'. To me the process is a bit like using brushes to uncover an archaeological find; it is fine work, but what is underneath is hugely important even if it is only a fragment. Perhaps most profound, however, is that in sharing The Journeys I think I have learned about the possibilities of real courage.

Notes

1. First published in the 1996 No.4 issue of the *Dulwich Centre Newsletter.* Republished here with permission.

2. We share a history of beginning our professional lives as teachers and discovering that our interests lay with the young people we met, rather than with the content we were meant to be teaching them. This led us both into training as school counsellors with jobs that now allow us to spend all day having interesting conversations with young people and their families. Although we have quite different approaches to our lives and work, in the six years we have worked together at Selwyn College, Auckland, New Zealand, we have developed a wonderful sense of togetherness in our shared values and beliefs about the work we are doing - not to mention a love of fun, laughter, and café lattes in the local café. Dorothea and Aileen can be contacted c/- Selwyn College, Auckland, New Zealand.

3. The students whose voices appear in this paper have chosen to remain anonymous.

4. The Challenge Ropes Course is run by Liz Penman, a Project Adventure trainer.

5. A *powhiri* is a formal Maori ceremony of welcome which follows traditional protocol.

Reference

White, M. & Epston, D. 1990: *Narrative Means to Therapeutic Ends.* New York: W.W.Norton.

PART IV

Working
with
Communities

In October 1995, Dulwich Centre Publications was introduced, through video-tape[1], to forms of community work developed in response to the HIV/AIDS epidemic in Malawi. This video-tape was made in Africa by a group of Malawian workers who describe themselves as CARE counsellors[2], and a Dutch Aid worker, Yvonne Sliep. The tape demonstrated a community orientated approach that sought to facilitate unity in the face of HIV/AIDS. This was an approach that potentially could be applied to other overwhelming problems.

This video has now caused many ripples in other communities. For example, here in South Australia, Barb Wingard, of the Aboriginal Women's Health and Healing Project, has created a number of programs inspired by the ideas of the CARE counsellors. A video-tape of this work has been made[3] and has recently attracted interest in other countries.

This next paper, '*Pang'ono pang'ono ndi mtolo* - little by little we make a bundle', seeks to describe aspects of the work of the CARE counsellors. This section is not intended to convey ready-made answers to complex problems. Nor does it attempt to explore all the complexities of working with issues of HIV/AIDS in Malawi. Instead it is hoped that it will encourage others to explore new ways of working with communities that are facing potentially overwhelming problems, ways of working that build upon unity and traditional knowledges, and that prioritise community participation and accountability at the local level. Following this paper, Yvonne Sliep has included some notes in relation to externalizing problems in a community or group context.

Barb Wingard, in her papers 'Introducing "sugar"' and 'Grief: Remember, reflect, reveal', then tells the story of how some Indigenous Australians have been encouraged by, and have built upon, the ideas of the CARE counsellors. Barb describes the development of approaches to two issues central to Indigenous Australian communities: diabetes and grief. Again, these stories are not intended as ready-made answers or prescriptions, but instead they are offered as invitations to others to imagine ways of working with communities that build upon cultural knowledges and histories, and that create the opportunity to bring difficult topics out into the open.

It is hoped that giving these stories and invitations a broader audience will result in further ripples and other creative interpretations of this work.

Notes

1. This video-tape is entitled: 'Mr AIDS, Mrs CARE, Malemia 2' (August 1995), CARE counsellors, Malawi.

2. CARE is an acronym for Community Action Renders Enablement.

3. This video tape is entitled: 'Sugar.' (1996) Aboriginal Women's Health & Healing Project, South Australia.

8

Pang'ono pang'ono ndi mtolo -
Little by little we make a bundle[1]

The work of the CARE Counsellors
& Yvonne Sliep[2]

Conversations with AIDS and CARE

The following dialogue is an example of the conversations that have recently taken place in a number of villages in rural Malawi. After extensive consultation, the chiefs of certain villages have invited CARE counsellors into their communities to talk about HIV/AIDS. The CARE counsellors have developed a particular way of facilitating these conversations. One worker plays the role of Mr/Mrs AIDS, who represents HIV/AIDS; and another plays the role of Mr/Mrs CARE, who represents the community. Members of the village are invited to ask questions of these two characters, and a conversation develops. These conversations are spoken in Chichewa, the local language, and are often held outside in the shade of trees. The conversations are accompanied by drama and song, and invariably the atmosphere is one of curiosity, open heartedness and laughter.

Asking questions of AIDS

Villagers: *Who are you? Who are your parents?*

Mr/Mrs AIDS: *My name AIDS is an acronym. I am Acquired Immune Deficiency Syndrome. Originally, when I'm just starting out, I begin as a virus. My parents are HIV: Human Immune-deficiency Virus. I start as this virus and then grow to become AIDS.*

Villagers: *Why did you decide to enter our lives? What are your hopes and dreams?*

Mr/Mrs AIDS: *My hopes and dreams are to destroy the human race and to wipe out this nation.*

Villagers: *Why do you like our country so much, why do you like Africa?*

Mr/Mrs AIDS: *This is a very good environment for me. There is poverty. There are a lot of people. There is hunger. Why wouldn't I come here? In the midst of all these problems I find my way in. I will stay here. Perhaps I will stay here forever. Africa is my rejoicing continent!* [laughter]

Villagers: *How do you manage to get inside a person's life?*

Mr/Mrs AIDS: *Whenever I am accepted into a person's body: through intercourse, through blood, or through piercing - whenever I am given a chance I move in.*

Villagers: *And once you are inside, what effect do you have on someone who is infected by you?*

Mr/Mrs AIDS: *I have several effects when I get inside a person. I affect the person spiritually, mentally and physically. I try to destroy their immune system. Once it is gone I find it easy to make myself bigger, to multiply. I make them very sick. Sometimes it takes me a while, but generally I make them very sick and they die.*

Villagers: *What effects do you have on our households, on our families?*

Mr/Mrs AIDS: *I have a philosophy of divide and rule. When I enter a household I disorganise the family. I make all kinds of problems. I am disunity and arguments.*

Villagers: *You must be very rude.*

Mr/Mrs AIDS: *I tell you, I am terrible.*

Villagers: *What effect do you have on our communities?*

Mr/Mrs AIDS: *If I get into the community I disorganise it. I disorganise the chiefs, the people - you who sit around me now. I create conflict so that you cannot contain me. I overwhelm people so that they sit around thinking about me. I make them feel hopeless.*

Villagers: *What are the things that you do to keep yourself strong? What conditions are favourable for you to work in?*

Mr/Mrs AIDS: *I have several favourable conditions. Where people are divided and confused I work well. You see, I am sneaky. I also like situations where people in the village are drinking. They can't see me but I am there. When girls are playing with the boys, I am there. If people forget about me, if they don't look after themselves, if they do not use condoms, then I get my chance and I take it.*

Villagers: *I have a more specific question for you. Do you think a woman who is infected should have another child?*

Mr/Mrs AIDS: *Oh yes, as many children as she can - that way I'll be very famous.*

Villagers: *What about the husbands? Do you think if a husband is infected he should tell his wife?*

Mr/Mrs AIDS: *No way. No way. I'm sneaky. I like secrecy. I don't like people getting together to talk about me. I don't like gatherings like this one. When you tell each other about me it gets in my way. I don't want any of this opposition.*

Asking questions of CARE

Villagers: *And who are you? Where do you come from? Who are your parents?*

Mr/Mrs CARE: *I come from here. I am your mother. I am your father. I am your grandparents, your child, your sister, your brother. I am you. I am this community so you are my parents. Our histories have created me.*

Villagers: *Why have you come to us now?*

Mr/Mrs CARE: *I see that you have met Mr/Mrs AIDS. I have come now so that we can work together, to get rid of this menace, to take care of the people who are already sick. That's why I have come.*

Villagers: *What are your hopes and dreams?*

Mr/Mrs CARE: *AIDS has come to destroy us and has brought a lot of suffering. My hope is that we will overcome AIDS through unity. By working together, I dream that we will lessen the suffering of the families and communities.*

Villagers: *How will we do this? For instance, how will we support the orphans?*

Mr/Mrs CARE: *We will remember our histories. During the older days our ancestors were also dealing with orphans. In those days, the relatives, the sisters, brothers, the uncles, aunts, would take care of the orphans. That is community. Similarly now, through unity, if the relatives unite we will find ways of assisting those whose parents have died.*

Villagers: *But it's not always as easy as that. I have a sister. She has been going about with men, living in bars. We tried to discourage her behaviour but she wasn't responding to our appeals. Now it appears as if she is sick and everyone is pointing fingers, saying she is eating the fruits of her past behaviour. Should we still assist her?*

Mr/Mrs CARE: *She is one part of us. Community is made up of everyone. She is sick, that means part of our whole body is sick. We must help this sister of yours. She might be thinking that she does not deserve it. Her spirit may be crumbling. We need to give her some hope. Maybe not for this life but for the next.*

Villagers: *But how will we overcome AIDS? How can we make people understand that they can help?*

Mr/Mrs CARE: *Through action. If we do things together they will begin to understand. If we can assist this man to look after his sister, others will notice. If each one of us is doing something then we will be able to share our problems. Do you remember that AIDS said: 'I hate unity. I like to go around disorganising the community, the family'? If we unite as a community, as a family, Mr/Mrs AIDS won't have any room to come between us.*

Villagers: *Where does your power and strength come from?*

Mr/Mrs CARE: *In order to answer that, let me tell you about the bundle of sticks.* (Slowly Mr/Mrs CARE picks up a stick, a piece of wood from nearby trees known by the local people to be magical. With the stick in hand, Mr/Mrs CARE turns and offers it to the nearest person and asks them to use their strength to break it. The first person cannot, and so the stick is passed slowly and quietly. Finally it cracks and breaks in two.)

One stick on its own is easily broken. (Removing the broken stick, Mr/Mrs CARE turns and picks up a bundle of sticks, also from the magic trees, but this time bound together by twine. The villagers are invited to try to break the bundle. This time they cannot.)

One stick on its own is easily broken, but, if you put sticks in a bundle, that bundle becomes very strong, so strong that you cannot break it. A spirit on its own can be easily broken. But bundled together we will not break. That is our power and our strength. Pang'ono pang'ono ndi mtolo - *little by little we must make a bundle.*

Reflecting on talking with AIDS and CARE

The exercise is very powerful. AIDS first came into Malawi in 1985. Since then we have been lecturing villagers about the dangers of HIV/AIDS but we haven't really known whether they were interested, what they knew, or whether they even wanted us to be lecturing them. In the Mr/Mrs AIDS and Mr/Mrs CARE setting, the people in the villages have a chance to ask us questions. If they have doubts, it's their turn to express them. They ask us questions and it becomes a real conversation. (Charles Kachala, in conversation, 1996)

Charles Kachala, is a medical clinician at Chiradzulu General Hospital in southern Malawi, has played the character of Mr/Mrs AIDS in the communities he works with. He has found that inviting the villagers into conversations with HIV/AIDS creates the context for a meaningful exchange of information and knowledge. At the same time the real concerns of the community can be brought out into the open, and a forum for dialogue over these concerns is created. Most importantly, perhaps, is that space is created for the community to join together against the problem of AIDS. Issues that may have been dividing the village begin to be seen as a consequence of AIDS, rather than the fault of individuals, and this increases the possibility of collective action. Rather than the focus remaining on AIDS and the problems which face the community, the introduction of Mr/Mrs CARE allows the villagers to identify what it is that they value most. This assists them to articulate the strengths, knowledges and historical traditions which they can build upon as they organise themselves in their struggle against HIV/AIDS. As Mr/Mrs CARE constantly refers questions back to the community, space is created to remember and honour histories of collective care and support within the village.

Consultation

These conversations about HIV/AIDS can only occur after extensive periods of consultation with the chiefs and other members of the villages. Respectful consultation lays the foundations for the conversations to take place within the context of openness and trust.

As a result of consultative processes, within the work of the CARE counsellors of Malawi, the character of AIDS has generally been played by a man, i.e. Mr AIDS, and the character of CARE has generally been played by a woman, i.e. Mrs CARE. It is felt by the local people that this arrangement is appropriate and works successfully in their context. Experiences of gender, AIDS, and sexuality, vary enormously across different contexts, and these variations affect meanings and inform particular ways of working. Some communities, both within Malawi and elsewhere, have facilitated this exercise with AIDS and CARE played interchangeably by men and women.

The ripples of conversations with AIDS and CARE

The following pages contain examples of the directions in which these conversations have been taken in some villages. These examples are not intended to give more than an impression of what is a fluid and changing process. They are included to illustrate potential avenues that are opened when villagers begin to speak directly with Mr/Mrs AIDS and Mr/Mrs CARE.

Creating space for difficult questions

Inviting the villagers into conversations with AIDS and CARE can provide the opportunity for dilemmas to be raised. Mrs Chinguwo, who has often played the character of Mrs CARE, reflects on this:

> *The women often ask me 'How can we as a team defeat AIDS?' or 'If someone is sick how can we as a group in the community care for them?' Sometimes the questions are much more complicated. Today a woman asked a question about an unfaithful husband. Actually she said: 'Suppose you are married and your husband is away and you don't know what he is doing. Suppose he has been away for quite a while and you'd like to have some sexual contact because you've been on your own for too long. How could you go about that?'*
>
> *That was a very bold question to ask, especially for a woman in our culture in front of men, in front of boys and girls. I think they are worried and they want to find a way of solving these problems. It was very, very bold of her. I think the exercise in some way assisted.* (Mrs Chinguwo, in conversation, 1996)

Caucusing over plans of action

At times, after Mr/Mrs CARE has told the story of the bundle of sticks, the villagers are invited to group themselves into caucuses:

The women group together, the girls together, the boys together and the men together, so that they can discuss issues on their own. Traditionally when you have everyone together, the women and children do not talk, they can not voice their opinions. On the other hand when the boys and the girls are together, the boys dominate. We would rather have the real opinions from different age groups and different sexes. We ask them to come up with strategies to deal with Mr/Mrs AIDS. Facilitators go with each group and we invite them to discuss what they think they can do to overcome Mr/Mrs Aids. (Howard Kasiya, in conversation, 1996)

The caucuses are often particularly important when issues of control, power and sexuality are to be discussed:

Usually when I talk with rural women and you mention condoms they will shy away. But some women today spoke out and said that if they brought condoms into their homes their husbands would literally chase them out. So they still haven't got control over their own lives. They might want to use condoms but they do not have the power to say so. It's a big problem. (Mrs Chinguwo, in conversation, 1996)

In the younger women's caucuses, the issue of prostitution and sex for sustenance is often articulated:

Those young girls in school from poor families, who do not have enough money for food, for soap, are often approached by somebody with money, who says: 'I love you, I'll marry you, here is 100 Kwacha [Malawian dollars]*'. The next time the man takes the girl to his house it is very difficult for her to refuse as he is her source of income for the family. These men have decided that most of the women are HIV positive so they are going for the youth in the belief that the youth are clean.* (Charles Kachala, in conversation, 1996)

Caucuses allow issues like these to be spoken about. Having discussed the issues that they feel are most important, and having developed their own ideas as to action that can be taken, the groups then return and report back. Their plans of action are often documented for future reference.

Election

When the village comes together again we build on what they decided in their own groups. We ask them to decide whether they support Mr/Mrs AIDS or Mr/Mrs CARE. (Howard Kasiya, in conversation, 1996)

At times the community is given the opportunity to take a stand (literally) to support either Mr/Mrs AIDS or Mr/Mrs CARE. An election of sorts takes place and, inevitably, the community rises and stands alongside Mr/Mrs CARE. At this point the CARE counsellors begin to sing and the villagers join. It is a song of unity and strength. A wall of music and a wall of bodies is formed, walls that Mr/Mrs AIDS cannot get through. Mr/Mrs AIDS is left on the outer - alone. Through the use of drama, laughter and song, Mr/Mrs AIDS is then bustled, cajoled and danced out of the village (see photograph on page 4).

Mr/Mrs CARE: *We can see that Mr/Mrs AIDS could find no way in. There is no room for AIDS to come between us. Why? Because we have united together, just like this bundle* [holding the sticks to the sky]. *If we unite like this bundle we can overcome AIDS.*

Mr/Mrs CARE then hands to each of the villagers one of the sticks that together made up the bundle (see photograph on page 3).

Mr/Mrs CARE: *In order to remember this feeling of unity, I am going to give you a stick each. Whenever we need hope we will remember that we are working together. We will remember that with one stick you can make only a small fire. It can easily be put out. But with many sticks we can make the whole bush burn.*

From suffering to courage - a new identity for the village

The CARE counsellors often try to facilitate conversations that allow for the villagers to reconsider their views of their own community. One way this is done is to invite Mr/Mrs AIDS and Mr/Mrs CARE to share their reflections on the particular village community.

Villagers: *Mr/Mrs AIDS how do you see this community?*

Mr/Mrs AIDS: *I'm convinced that, all in all, this community is trying to unite. It is trying to put all its effort into destroying me. I am afraid I may have to decide not to stay here much longer. I am looking for a community that is disorganised, weak, where people do not know about me, a village where the leadership is poor. The way they are united here, the effort they have shown, I will probably have to leave sooner than I had expected.*

Villagers: *Mr/Mrs CARE how do you see this community?*

Mr/Mrs CARE: *It seems to me that this community understands the dangers of AIDS and the ways in which AIDS works. It seems that this village is ready to get rid of AIDS through uniting and working together. It is a very strong and determined community. It seems to be showing courage, willingness to work, and motivation. These things scare AIDS and drive it away.*

The facilitators are keen to open up space for the community to move from an identity associated with suffering to one associated with courage. They explore with the villagers how it felt to listen to both Mr/Mrs AIDS and Mr/Mrs CARE. They speculate as to what could happen if the village held onto the feeling of unity that occurred when the bundle of sticks was held to the sky.

Plans of action

In order to develop plans of action, the facilitators explore the ways in which Mr/Mrs AIDS is getting into the particular community and the steps that could be taken to prevent them. One example is in the area of traditional healing practices. As Charles Kachala, a medical clinician at Chiradzulu General Hospital, explains below, traditional healers have much to offer Western medicine. At the same time, however, he fears that some of their methods may be contributing to HIV infection:

Most people here believe in traditional healers, although some people due to Christian religious beliefs do not go to them. We work here with traditional healers. That's why there was a traditional healer's association formed. We understand that traditional healers are here and will always be here. They use needles for tattoos so we are talking with them about how they are going to prevent AIDS. We also want to talk with them about their beliefs. There is a research unit for traditional healers to understand how some of the herbs they use are very helpful in preventing illness. As colleagues, we are slowly beginning to understand each other.

It is not uncommon for a man to be bewitched - I've been bewitched so many times - that now we have to have protection, in the form of tattoos. Other people wear it or take it. Magic is here. Traditional healers are here. They come to the hospital if we need them, but usually people will go to them in the community.

We share what we think we should leave for them and what we think they should leave for us. We explain to them how not to spread the virus. If they are using one razor blade for tattoos on so many people, then, on top of doing good work, they may also be spreading the virus. So really we are beginning to work hand-in-hand throughout the country. (Charles Kachala, in conversation, 1996)

These partnerships are especially important in areas where Western medicine is inaccessible to most of the population:

The majority of the population [in Malawi] *rely on traditional medicine - the reasons for this include its convenience. Traditional medicines are available in most villages - saving people from walking long distances, waiting in queues and then perhaps receiving little or nothing as medicines are often in short supply in health centres. The cost of traditional medicine is more affordable and often offers a way of payment adapted to suit the recipient.* (Mthobwa & Brugha 1995)

In order to raise with traditional healers the issue of transferring HIV through tattooing, Mr/Mrs CARE might ask them about the influence of Mr/Mrs AIDS on their work and lives:

Mr/Mrs CARE: *Mr/Mrs AIDS says he is going to use you to destroy our community. He is saying he is going to use you as traditional healers. What are we going to do? How do you think he'll try to use you?*

Traditional healers: *He will use one of us first to split us. He will say 'Don't listen to the others, I am the best, I use my own razor'. How are we going to respond to such a person, to such a situation?*

Mr/Mrs CARE: *We will have to find ways of staying united.*

Mr/Mrs AIDS: *That might work for a while, but people are going to get tired and I'll jump on in again.*

These sorts of conversations continue until specific plans are developed for current problems and for those that are forecast. This occurs in each of the caucus groups. The structure of these dialogues keeps the community united and the problem clearly located as Mr/Mrs AIDS.

Ceremony

To bring the day's work to an end, on some occasions a ceremony is held. These take the form of rituals in which the plans of action are added to the documents that record the reflections on the strengths of the community. These are documents of hope, testimonies of unity and strength, and plans for the future. They are officially handed over to the chief of the village at the end of the ceremony.

Mr/Mrs CARE: *These documents alongside the bundle of sticks will be here to remind you. They can be consulted whenever they are needed. They can be used to summon up a sense of unity and to remind you of your plans.*

Umodzi ndi mphamvu - unity is a sign of strength

By personifying the problem of AIDS and providing a focus for uniting the community (Mr/Mrs CARE), the CARE counsellors are providing the opportunity for villagers to get more in contact with their own histories of caring and collective action. Through caucusing, the voices of all members of the community are sought out and their ideas documented. Through asking questions of Mr/Mrs AIDS and Mr/Mrs CARE about their views of the day's events, the village is provided with powerful reflections of their collective identity - one of strength and courage in the face of HIV/AIDS. Importantly, the ideas about how AIDS can be overcome are generated by the community itself, and new sorts of conversations begin to take place around these ideas, as Yvonne Sliep[1] describes:

This work has offered me hope because dialogue seems to begin between the community and Mr/Mrs AIDS and then spread to conversations between community members and with community workers. I have watched as villagers have begun to separate themselves from the problem of AIDS, and the stigma surrounding the illness has then begun to decrease. At the same time, these ways of working change the relationship between us as workers and the community. We cease to be acting on the community and instead we begin to work together, united against the problem of AIDS.

Perhaps most hopeful to me has been to witness a reduction in conflict and division, and to watch the sense of failure being replaced with a sense of energy and hopefulness. To see potentially despairing conversations about AIDS replaced by drama and song and by conversations of curiosity and laughter has been, for me, very powerful. (Yvonne Sliep, in conversation, 1997)

Perhaps the most important outcomes are those of community unity and a greater connection with cultural traditions of collective care:

It is a new thing in Malawi for a person to eat from their own plate. Culturally in Malawi we have a very big basin of food which everybody picks from. We live communally. Doing things together starts from our experiences in our families. The counselling that we were doing was taking us away from these traditions, away from our own culture. Now we are developing new ways. This type of counselling is bringing us back. It is saying: if we can share food in a basin together, if we can eat together and everybody has a share, if we can live collectively, without each of us having a plate, without the individualism - why can't we try a similar united, collective approach with problems like diseases which have no medicine? We are going back to what we know. It is empowering. It is giving the people in the family or those people in the community responsibility for the issue. It is giving them the powers so that they can assist their own people. (McDonald Suwande, in conversation, 1996)

Pang'ono pang'ono ndi mtolo - Little by little we make a bundle.

Notes

1. First published in the 1996 No.3 issue of the *Dulwich Centre Newsletter*. Republished here with permission.

2. CARE is an acronym that stands for Community Action Renders Enablement. The CARE counselling model was developed by Yvonne Sliep after four years' research in Malawi as a cultural sensitive counselling model for HIV/AIDS. It is currently used as the national strategy for AIDS Counselling.

3. Yvonne was born in South Africa and currently lives in the Netherlands. Africa, where she has worked most of her life, forms a deep part of her being and greatly influences the way she sees and lives in the world. Most of her experience with narrative work has been with groups and communities where people more often relate to 'We' than to 'I'. For Yvonne, creating ways together with others to prevent Problems causing confusion and divisions between 'us' and 'them' has been challenging. Working with the strength and ability of groups of people has been inspiring and energising.

   Yvonne would love to share ideas with others, and can be contacted at: s' Gravensloot 31(b), 3471 BP Kamerik, The Netherlands, email: y-sliep@wirehub.nl

Externalizing problems
in a community or group context

a note from

Yvonne Sliep

The preceding article described an attempt to externalize and personify the problem of HIV/AIDS within a community setting in rural Malawi, Africa. We have found that creating the context for communities to directly interview Mr/Mrs AIDS has:

- reduced blaming practices and broken the debilitating silence created by stigma;
- reduced feelings of failure and isolation;
- stimulated dialogue within the community and also between the community and community workers;
- changed the situation away from one in which the community was being acted upon by both the problem and the community workers, to one in which the community and community workers are united against the problem;
- created the opportunity for community members to ask questions free from guilt or shame;
- enabled ideas of how to counteract the problem to be generated from the community itself rather than be imposed from the outside (this greatly reduces the possibility of being set up for failure).

Creating the possibility for the community to then interview a counterplot of CARE or UNITY has further:

- opened up possibilities for action,
- encouraged co-operation and unity,
- highlighted people's ability and skills to take action against the effects of the problem, and
- increased a sense of hope and inspiration.

In our experience in Malawi, problems tend to be enigmatic and try to amuse the crowd. Because of this, when trying to externalize a problem in a group setting, care needs to be taken that the problem does not get too much attention and energy. If it is a problem that uses stigmatisation to divide people (as does AIDS), extra care needs to be taken to ensure that the conversation in no way increases the stigma towards those within the group or community who have AIDS.

The conversation described in the preceding paper is only one part of a broader process. Community conversations require careful planning and follow-up. Involvement of the group or community in the planning, implementation, follow-up, and evaluation of the process, are all a part of developing respectful processes of accountability.

The process described involved reclaiming a collective identity of unity, despite the divisive nature of AIDS. Everyone in the community was invited into this reclamation. We quickly learnt how AIDS tries to infiltrate communities through the most vulnerable. This meant that women and young people were actively included in the process. By exploring unique outcomes - times when UNITY was prevailing over AIDS - the community was able to witness and build upon richly described stories of community strength and connectedness. These conversations are continuing.

9

Introducing 'sugar'[1]

by

Barbara Wingard [2]

I'd like to tell the story of 'Sugar' because to me it is a story of trying to find new ways of working, of trying different things, taking new steps. In early 1996, as a member of the Aboriginal Women's Health and Healing Project,[3] I had the opportunity to watch a video of the work of the CARE counsellors of Malawi.

The ten of us involved in the Aboriginal Women's Health and Healing Project really enjoyed watching this video. It really touched me very strongly and I couldn't wait to come home and work with the ideas. I specifically thought about how this sort of work could be used with diabetes as it is an illness that is causing a lot of harm within Aboriginal communities. Not long before watching the video, a doctor had asked us here at Murray Mallee Community Health Centre to organise something for three people who were very sick with diabetes and constantly coming into hospital.

I said to Jenny Baker, who was one of the other members of the

Aboriginal Women's Health and Healing Project, 'Jenny, wouldn't this be fantastic to use with diabetes?' And she said, 'Yeah Barb, we should do it together'. We went away from that day with a sense of excitement, with a feeling of, 'Wow, we've got to use this'. I couldn't wait to get to Murray Bridge, where I work, to try it.

I developed an exercise which I first of all showed to the other members of the Aboriginal Women's Health and Healing Project. It worked very well and I couldn't wait to give it to the people. That was going to be the big test.

Setting the scene

In the exercise I played the role of diabetes or 'Sugar'. I carefully set the scene in ways that I felt were culturally appropriate. As an Aboriginal person I knew that it would be wrong to put other Aboriginal people on the spot, or single people out. To avoid this I came up with a number of questions that I gave to the participants which they could ask me and I would respond. The participants were very happy to start by asking these simple little questions I had already come up with. If I had expected them to come up with their own questions straight away it might have been difficult to get people to participate. Giving them questions took away the uncomfortableness. I had hoped that after they had asked me these set questions that a general conversation would begin, and this is what happened. At the end people came up with their own questions that they would have been afraid to ask at the beginning.

I had been impressed at the way the CARE counsellors of Malawi had invited communities into conversations with one character representing AIDS: Mr/Mrs AIDS, and one character representing community care: Mr/Mrs CARE. As I was doing this work on my own I only developed the one character: 'Sugar'. I thought it would be too complicated for me to play two characters, although I had seen how well this had worked in the video from Malawi. Just having the one character, 'Sugar', meant that she had to be very versatile. She spoke of the ways she was affecting people, but also at times played the role of an educator.

Perhaps we will explore using two characters later on - who knows what future directions will hold. This is just a starting point. It's not perfect. I wouldn't want to put it across as perfect. It is just to give people ideas. I want people to go off and develop their own ways of working. If it came across as perfect it could scare people - expectations might get too high. Every situation is different and every community is different. I'd like everyone to have the freedom to develop things in their own way.

Talking to 'sugar'

The group: *Who are you?*

Sugar: *My name is diabetes but a lot of people call me Sugar. You can call me Sugar. I can be anybody's disease but I do my best work with Nungas[4] because they can't quite control me yet.*

There was a man in the group and when I said they could all call me Sugar it created a lot of laughter!

The group: *How do you work?*

Sugar: *It's my job to make sure you don't get enough insulin or none at all. Most people know about my condition. I'm very popular and I'm all over the world - I'm pretty sure of having a job until I retire. Years ago it was hard for me to get a job with you people because there were great hunters who lived off the land, good tucka [food] and plenty of exercise. You people were healthy.*

At this stage I referred to a poster about 'healthy bodies' that I made for the program.

Now though, thanks to this thing called urban living, you have heaps of shops to go to and are tempted by the smell of food, by television, books that always show cakes, chocolates and fatty foods. You have very little exercise. All this just makes me so happy.

The group: *How different are you from a healthy body?*

Sugar: *To explain that I need to introduce you to my family. I come from very strong kin relationships as I know you do. Aboriginal people have strong family relationships and I totally rely on my blood relatives.*

There's my Mother Heart - without her I'm a goner, and three sets of twins - Cousin Kidneys, Cousin Pili's [eyes] and Cousin Feet except they're not here today - gone walkabout. My main man is a gland called Pancreas. This is where I do my best work. I affect all these parts of the body - all my relatives. This is what makes me different from a healthy body.

At this point I refer to a poster about 'unhealthy bodies'.

The group: *What don't you like about your job?*

Sugar: *Well I come in two types of diabetes and I don't like this part of my job. I have to remember the families that have my history.*

First of all there is Type 1, or Juvenile Onset Diabetes. My work here is usually with young people below the age of thirty, but it can happen at any age. With Type 1, the pancreas produces no insulin because the cells that make it have been destroyed by the white cells of the body. People therefore require insulin injections to control their blood glucose levels.

Then there is Type 2, or Mature Onset Diabetes. This usually happens in people who are over 40 years old and especially if they are overweight. Type 2 often responds to diet, appropriate exercise and weight reduction, but sometimes tablets and then later, insulin, may be required.

I would give out a handout at this point.

The group: *What makes you powerful?*

Sugar: *I become powerful when people are shamed, divided, and isolated. I become powerful when people are overweight, including pregnant women with big babies; when Nungas over 40 never get their eyes tested, neglect sores, don't eat properly, don't use medication and injections, don't visit diabetic clinics or programs, don't have blood pressures taken, never have urine tests; when they do no exercise; and when they stay home and away from people who know about me.*

The group: *What weakens you?*

Sugar: *It weakens me when Aboriginal people have a chance to ask questions, to talk together in their own ways. It weakens me when people are no longer alone, when they stand together. Other things also weaken me - people taking responsibility for their own health, weight loss, diets, blood pressure checks, foot care, trachoma clinics, people controlling their blood sugar glucose levels. All these things weaken me.*

As Sugar answers what weakens her she becomes weaker and weaker until she is almost under the table!

Different conversations

What we got out of it was quite magical. The most important thing was that, after we had been through these questions and answers, the participants started asking their own questions of Sugar. The conversations afterwards went on for an hour and a half, just discussing the issues that came up. The exercise seemed to lead to the possibility of people asking their own questions, questions that they had never felt free to ask before, and this led to new sorts of conversations.

It was obvious by the end that some people had never understood diabetes before. Maybe professional people had tried to explain and they'd been too ashamed to say 'I don't know' or, 'I don't understand'. I think we learned that we need to break diabetes down so that the people can understand.

When I asked one woman who is normally very quiet what she thought of the poster she said, 'I'd never understood what Sugar was about. That's given me a real vision.' She wasn't responding to me, she wasn't responding to the diabetic sister or the dietitian, she was responding to Sugar. It was just so different. It wasn't about me, Barb, it was because she could have a direct conversation with Sugar. Another woman was giving herself injections and she was wondering why it was so difficult. She wasn't moving the needles from place to place. We talked and talked. At the end of it I just went 'like wow!' (thumbs up)

Humour

It was really good to play Sugar. I am naturally a bit of a clown, and for a lot of Aboriginal people that is our survival tool - our humour, our joking. To create that sort of environment with Sugar was really good. They really loved it.

It was because of the humour that they were able to pick it up better. The male who was there, when he sees me walking down the street, he still says, 'Here comes Sugar!' It's really rippled.

Curiosity

The relationship of the participants to Sugar was one of curiosity. Anger didn't creep in at all even when Sugar was extremely boastful. At times Sugar said really, really awful things like: 'If you don't look after your feet you'll get sores and your limbs can drop off'. After I said it I felt quite awful for saying it, but it wasn't me, it was Sugar speaking.

I think using imagery of weakening or strengthening Sugar was better than showing aggression. The idea of asking 'what makes you strong?' 'what weakens you?' was an excellent idea from the Malawi video. When Sugar was answering the question 'what weakens you?' she actually started to go down, to wilt. It was making her weak. When I ran the program here I actually got under the table - it weakened Sugar so much.

Professional relations with 'sugar'

It was wonderful to see how the other health professionals entered into a relationship with Sugar. They started to call me Sugar, and to ask questions of Sugar. To see professional people come into it and accept this whole new process, I think that warmed me the most. The diabetic sister now uses 'Sugar' in some form with mainstream clients. They have also been using the video that we made with other health professionals. The podiatrists send me very positive feedback on coloured pieces of paper in the shape of little feet! I send my notes back in black, yellow and red - Nunga coloured feet!

Culture

I wanted to bring in some cultural aspects so that they could really relate to Sugar, so they felt they belonged to Sugar. Otherwise it would have been far too mainstream and that's often the problem with other programs. That's why our people are getting lost because often there are no attempts to talk about these things in culturally appropriate ways. By talking about our people's history, we made the link between them and Sugar.

I tried to make the exercise culturally appropriate. By giving them the questions first meant that everyone was a part of the process in a non-threatening way. By not using jargon, people felt that we were all speaking the same language.

I think that often Aboriginal people have felt shamed at asking questions, or that Sugar is just too complicated to understand. The way the questions were given reduced shame - they became a part of talking with Sugar. The fact that we were talking about Nungas and our history and our culture also reduced shame.

Togetherness

Perhaps the biggest thing that reduces shame is doing something all together - breaking down the isolation. Sugar is just one of many issues facing Aboriginal people's lives. This offered a different way of seeing Sugar. They looked at Sugar that day as something that should be taken notice of, something that is affecting the Aboriginal community. It's a community problem. If it's not affecting you it's affecting your grandmother, uncle or aunty. Every family is effected by diabetes, one way or another. By all talking with Sugar it gave the feeling that together we need to take notice, and that together we can take action.

Notes

1. First published in the 1996 No.3 issue of the *Dulwich Centre Newsletter*. Republished here with permission.

2. Barbara is the proud mother of three grown-up adults, is blessed with eight grandchildren, and is fortunate to have her elderly mother living with her. When not working, Barbara enjoys being with her grannies [grandchildren], and her other passion is to be involved in narrative practices. Barbara can be contacted at the Murray Mallee Community Health Service, PO Box 346, Murray Bridge 5253, South Australia.

3. In 1994 funds were allocated from the South Australian Health Commission to the National Women's Health Program to assist in the area of health and healing. With these funds an Aboriginal Women's Health Forum was established which in turn initiated the Aboriginal Women's Health and Healing Project. This project involves ten Aboriginal women from different areas within South Australia - Maggie Charles from Berri, Leta Sullivan from Goodwood, Maureen Williams from Coober Pedy, Christine Franks from Coffin Bay, Jenny Baker from Torrensville, Rosie Howson from Greenacres, Barbara Wingard from Murray Bridge, Shirley Grocke from Blyth, Terry Stewart from Angle Park and Anna Caponi from Port Augusta.

    The Aboriginal Women's Health and Healing Project is currently exploring a wide range of issues including training and the development of culturally appropriate ways of working.

4. Nunga is an Aboriginal word which is widely used to describe Aboriginal people of South Australia.

Reference

'Reclaiming Our Stories: Reclaiming Our Lives.' *Dulwich Centre Newsletter*, 1995 No.1 (special issue).

10

Grief:
Remember, reflect, reveal [1]

by

Barbara Wingard [2]

Grief is an area that we have so much work to do on in the Aboriginal communities. It's hard for us to develop programs in a lot of areas, including talking about diabetes or heart disease, if there is so much grief in our communities. So many of our losses have been unjust and unacknowledged, and because of this they can be difficult to deal with, difficult to grieve. For a long time I have been interested in trying to find ways of talking with Aboriginal people about these issues.

At Camp Coorong (*Dulwich Centre Newsletter*, 1995 No.1) we talked a great deal about deaths in custody, the links between grief, loss and injustice and trying to find culturally appropriate ways forward. This year, issues of grief once again touched my own life when I heard about the West Terrace Project.

West Terrace Project

In our day if you had a stillborn baby, or a baby that died soon after birth, the health professionals would remove the baby and take care of all the arrangements. The mother often wouldn't even see the baby's body and they wouldn't know where the body was taken. The West Terrace Project has involved trying to find the location of the graves of these children. There had been many, many enquiries over the years about where the babies had been buried. Apparently there were so many enquiries that they found there were 30,000 babies supposed to be buried at West Terrace Cemetery. People wanted to know where. I was one of these mothers. I lost my son Michael shortly after his birth. I didn't know where he was buried and so I got involved in the West Terrace Project. I attended the ceremony of the unveiling of the Baby Memorial that is dedicated to all the lost children.

West Terrace Cemetery, Adelaide
Baby Memorial

Under a Bay tree, a small sitting space formed by a curved wall of quarried stone which directs attention to a symbolic bowl of water made of granite on which floats a broken chain of white daisies in bronze.

The water symbolises calm, the white daisies innocence and the broken chain - a life cut off. The plaques are in the shape of leaves set in ceramic tiles and the whole memorial is in the form of a carpet of bay leaves - bay leaves do not change when they fall.

(Extract from Dedication and Unveiling of the Baby Memorial. West Terrace Cemetery, Adelaide, South Australia. Sunday, March 10th, 1996)

When I went to the ceremony at the West Terrace Cemetery I didn't see any Aboriginal women at the unveiling, and it bothered me. I thought that out of 30,000 babies there must be Aboriginal babies out there. Where were the people? That made me think that we need to get out there and talk, spread the word, share with them about the West Terrace Project. So I began to tell my story and send information out to other Aboriginal women.

Speaking out

As I was doing this I was asked to present at the Stillbirth and Neo Natal Deaths (SANDS) Conference. I agreed. I thought it would be an opportunity for me to share my story which would be healing for me, and I also wanted to tell the stories of Aboriginal people. I knew that I'd be the only Aboriginal person at the conference. I wished that there would be more of us but I also knew how daunting these conferences can be for me.

I decided to try to use my own grief as a way of joining. We all had that in common. I thought I could tell my own story of grief and then make the links to the broader stories of grief that we as Aboriginal people have experienced. I thought it might be healing for all of us. I began by telling my own story.

My story as an Aboriginal woman: The loss of a twin in the 1960s

Today I am going to share a part of my life with you and reflect on what it was like for me as a sixteen year old in the 1960s.

In those days we had an Aborigines Act where some Aboriginal people were given an Exemption which allowed us to mix with the wider community, but it also indicated that we ceased to be Aboriginal.

This act prevented many of my people from returning to their birth places on the missions. Also there was a loitering act which prevented people of many different races congregating together. This included mixing with our own people as well as our white friends.

In those days, we were not even citizens of this country. This didn't happen until 1967 when we could vote.

As a young girl growing up in these times I had a sense of not belonging and trying to hang on to my identity. During my school days I failed to fit in to the school system and spent my time in a special class till I was thirteen, and was able to get myself a job in a factory. It was good to get away from being called 'blacky' and 'dummy'. By this time I figured out that I didn't have anything in that head of mine but there wasn't anything wrong with my hands. By the time I was sixteen I felt like an old woman and fell in love and became pregnant ... even got married. But, like many Aboriginal women, I didn't like

Doctors and Hospitals. After all, I wasn't sick. Pregnancy to me wasn't a sickness, it was a natural condition.

After getting a bit of pressure from my mother to book into the hospital, I decided to go there seven months into my pregnancy. During the birth it was noticed that I was delivering twins, both boys. The first twin was 7lbs, the second was only 3lbs 14oz and he was breech, plus he had chest complications. I remember the joy of having two sons.

Two days later my son, Michael, passed away. I was young and death scared me and I wasn't encouraged to talk about it. The hospital took care of the burial which was to be at West Terrace Cemetery. There were no funeral services in those days. I had a baby to take home. My other son, Shawn, has been a constant reminder all these years and always will be, but that was the practice then - how times have changed!

Then early this year, I found out through the media about the project known as the Baby Memorial at West Terrace Cemetery which had been prompted by the requests of grieving mothers.

It was then that I was able to cry again. I couldn't believe that after all this time that I had unresolved grief. I felt disbelief - I am a Health Worker and know all about grief and the process... I couldn't help thinking about the mass graves. Going to the Baby Memorial Service was a great relief to me and my children.

After the service I needed to know where Michael's resting place was, but, following many enquiries, I found that he wasn't even at the West Terrace Cemetery!!!! At this stage I decided to write my story for other Aboriginal women and give them information and details of the West Terrace project.

A very special thankyou to the researchers at the West Terrace Cemetery, for their dedication and compassion for this project.

A happy ending for my story is that I have found out, finally, almost 32 years to the day, where my son is buried: the Cheltenham Cemetery was my son's last journey, his resting place.

Telling my story

Talking about my own story first was a bit emotional for me. I'd only just found out where Michael was buried. It was a bit emotional and that was clear in my voice. The Stillbirth and Neo Natal Death Support conference was a very moving time for a lot of women who had lost their babies. Women were finally talking. So many of us had been told not to, that it might upset us. A lot of the mothers who had lost their babies had been told: 'You've got to let go and move on now'. And that's the worst thing you can say. There is a lot of pressure to grieve in particular ways. We are trying to challenge this. We are trying to allow people to grieve in their own ways. Now we are talking, following it through.

My story was an old story, my loss. I used it as an indicator of how long grief can be with us. I also used that story to show that it wasn't just about my grief, that it's also about Aboriginal people and our 'griefs', all the different sorts of losses and injustices that we are trying to find our ways through.

At the SANDS conference there were no Aboriginal people except myself. I told my story in a way to let them know what it was like in the days when we weren't citizens of this country, when we couldn't vote. I told my story in these ways because we're always trying, us guys, always trying to get them to understand!

Telling my own story of grief was a way of joining with the non-Aboriginal people there. In some way I saw that grief could help us join - to create the context for us to talk through the broader losses. I wanted to talk about injustice in a healing way because, for us as Aboriginal people, telling the stories of injustice is a part of our grieving, a part of honouring our histories. Once I had told my story I thought, 'Okay that's my story. I've made the connection with the audience, now to move on, to let people know what it's like for us as Aboriginal people.'

Externalizing 'grief'

I had decided that I would try to play the character of 'Grief' and to invite the audience to ask me particular questions. I knew this would be very different to externalizing AIDS or Sugar, but I thought that it might help us to find common ground from where I could share the experiences of Aboriginal people. I wanted to make sure we could talk about our losses and injustices as Aboriginal people in a healing way. Playing the character of Grief and giving the participants questions to ask me was just a starting point. I'm telling this story in the hope that it will give people ideas that they could work on, so that they can come up with their own ways of working.

Talking with 'grief'

The group: *Have we met you before? What is your name?*

Grief: *Yes, you could have come across me sometime in your lives, in one way or another. My name is Grief and I'm the response to loss. I'm a process or a way of doing things.*

The group: *Has your presence been with Aboriginal People?*

Grief: *Yes and for a long time. To give you a good picture, allow me to take you on a Journey of Aboriginal History through some of the events in this country's past (loss of land, sickness, deaths, health, loss of language). You need to read in-between the lines for many happenings: removal of children, deaths in custody, rights and culture.*

At this point I put up a poster of the 'Journey of Aboriginal History' (see page 25) and encouraged people to fill in the gaps on the poster which I had left blank.

The group: *What's your way of doing things?*

Grief: *Let me talk about the different ways that people relate to me. I'm like stepping stones, and people step differently.*

When I spoke about stepping stones I talked in my own language and had a dialogue with the audience. I tried to talk about stepping stones from an Aboriginal perspective. One of the ways I did this was to focus on little griefs as with death all around us sometimes it is too overwhelming to talk about at first.

Aboriginal ways of grieving

Aboriginal people have their own ways of grieving. A part of Aboriginal people's story telling is that we hold onto our loved ones that aren't here any longer. It is a part of our history, who we belong to, who we are related to - our ancestors.

When an Aboriginal person meets another Aboriginal person we work out how we know each other through our relatives. We often refer to people who are no longer alive. Our old people are still very much with us. Through them we identify each other. I might not know your parents, but who were their parents? We constantly reflect and remember these people.

All my histories are through my grandmother. Everybody knows of her and her children. Hanging on to those old people is very much part of our strength. It is a part of our story-telling. They are talked about and so they are still with us.

When I talked about stepping stones it was with the hope that this metaphor would give a sense of movement, a sense of where people have been at and where they might move. We discussed the many different reactions people can have to loss. We talked about finding our own ways, our own individual ways, and our own cultural ways of grieving.

The group: *How close is loss to you?*

Grief: *Very close - we are partners. As I said before, Grief is the response to loss. Let me give you a definition of loss: 'It's something or someone you had or loved that has gone out of your lives'.*

People don't fully understand how broad loss is. Let me share with you the many different losses and you may be able to reflect on the Journey of Aboriginal History and the Journey of Grief.

At this point I tried to invite people to consider the losses and injustices that we as Aboriginal people have experienced and how we are trying to come to terms with these.

The group: *How can we deal with you?*

Grief: *There are many ways, people do it differently. Some people do it through having support available, talking about their grief, through maintaining spiritual and religious beliefs, through expressing feelings and stories - Men it's okay to cry. Some people help by gently encouraging the person to tell his/her own story, through listening far more than they talk. Never try to measure another person's grief. Their grief is what they say it is. Treat with love and respect any person who is grieving. Remember that every individual will grieve their own way.*

The beginnings of a conversation

It was a very moving experience. By starting on what we had in common it allowed me to share broader stories in a powerful way, a joined way. People were very open. It was wonderful to talk with the non-Aboriginal people afterwards. They were coming up to talk and hear more. I think it is good for non-Aboriginal people to hear these stories from Aboriginal people in the ways that we choose to tell them. It invites them to understand what has happened to Aboriginal people. It seemed as if a conversation had begun, a conversation that could be healing for all of us.

A different feeling

The session had a whole different feeling to Sugar (see *'Introducing Sugar'* this newsletter). Grief is such a sensitive issue so I did it in very different ways. I couldn't use humour. I couldn't be boastful. It was difficult as I had to shift from being silly and yet still get the message across. I love being boastful and silly and making people laugh. The humour was the one thing I did miss. Grief isn't a funny thing. It is a sad and delicate thing. We can't be laughing about it.

Honouring grief, talking together

I feel very close to Grief for lots and lots of reasons. I think the young children that we have now, the youth, really need to be in touch with our histories, including our histories of loss and how we have dealt with them. In some ways it is honouring of our grief. I wanted to get over to the people that grief is natural, normal, a thing that we have to go through. A lot of our people don't want to talk about Grief as we've had a lot of losses. Often it seems as if we are just moving from one death to another. Sometimes our people just get so weary. Sometimes it's just too much to go to one more funeral. We have to find ways of grieving together. It's far too hard to do on our own. I wanted us to look at Grief together, in a positive way, not a negative way but in a way that names the injustices, acknowledges our dead, and honours Aboriginal ways. I wanted to acknowledge that people grieve in different ways, and also to acknowledge the light at the end of the tunnel. I think the externalizing gave a little bit of a vision - that there's room to move on. That there are ways to deal with Grief together.

Grieving in our own ways

Aboriginal people have many different ways of dealing with grief. Often when people die there can be a good feeling that their spirit will be going with all the other spirits, other lost loved ones. A lot of Aboriginal people experience signs from loved ones who have died. Seeing particular birds, for instance, is often experienced as having ongoing contact with people who have died, ongoing contact with their spirits.

Some people feel that they have to move house after a person has died because their loved one's spirit still lives in the building. When I lost a loved one I needed to get the room in which he died blessed before I could re-enter it. There are a lot of different ways that Aboriginal people grieve. They can be quite complex.

I hope that the exercise and these ways of talking about grief puts people more in touch with their own ways of relating to death, to grief, to loss. I hope that it puts people more in touch with their own healing ways. I think telling the story of my own grief gives people a chance to relate to stories of loss and how differently they can be dealt with over time.

Reflecting on cultural histories

I am interested in using these ways of working with Aboriginal people. I think externalizing grief could invite people to reflect on their culture. A lot of programs don't reflect on Aboriginal culture and don't include our history. Many people are starting to forget about the invasion and the losses we have had: the land, the language, the culture. I want to talk about grief in ways that invite our people to reflect on our histories. Not to dwell on the past but to remember it, to look at some of the issues, some of the events in their lives, and see them as stepping stones. We need to talk about our history with our own people otherwise we are going to lose our young ones. They're going to have a lot of identity problems about where they belong and where they fit, and we have to help them. I think we do.

For Aboriginal people in some ways inviting people into conversations with Grief is inviting people to hold on. Grief invites us to cherish our people and histories. We need situations that invite us to be in touch with our histories to keep them alive. Talking about losses in these ways is one way of keeping our stories alive.

I'm trying to find ways for my people not to be angry, but, at the same time, I want us to understand our anger - deaths in custody, babies taken from families - there are many reasons. I want us to reflect on those histories - look at them as losses in our lives, and remember. Because we've started forgetting. Our culture is constantly being challenged, and this way our people can remember and reflect.

Grief and justice

It is important for us as Aboriginal people to make the links between justice and grief. So many of our losses have been unjust, and this is what is so hard to deal with. So many of our deaths are due to injustice. We are losing a lot of our people well before their time. A lot of our deaths are not natural deaths - for example, deaths in custody. It is tragic that we are losing our people so young. When my father died he was thirty-nine, a week off his fortieth birthday. To us that is a tragic event, but it is a common one. People like me, who are nearly fifty, we count our blessings that we are here each day. We say to each other how lucky we are to still be alive. We don't take life for granted.

We need the injustices addressed so that we can grieve our losses. We need stories told and acknowledged. Working on our grief in these ways is working towards justice.

Futures

I've been Sugar, I've been Grief. I can't wait for another one now - to see what it might be. There is so much work to be done at a grassroots level, and there are lots of other workers who are interested in building on this sort of work. It all blended in beautifully. And my own story of grief had a happy ending. I found my baby just before I went to the SANDS conference. A week before the conference they rang me up to tell me they had found him at Cheltenham Cemetery. So we're going to get a little plaque now. That's our next step - to have a family gathering to say goodbye to him, to honour him.

It was moving for me to find a way to be joined on issues of grief across cultures that got us talking together. It was also powerful to realise the links in my own life. There were many links for me between finding my way through my own losses and injustices, such as where my baby had been buried, and getting in touch with ways of working with Aboriginal communities on the injustices and losses we have all experienced. They were linked in some way. The link is there. I had to tell my story - to share it. We have to share our stories - to grieve and honour. We have to tell our stories in ways that make us stronger.

Notes

1. First published in the 1996 No.3 issue of the *Dulwich Centre Newsletter*. Republished here with permission.

2. Barbara is the proud mother of three grown-up adults, is blessed with eight grandchildren, and is fortunate to have her elderly mother living with her. When not working, Barbara enjoys being with her grannies [grandchildren], and her other passion is to be involved in narrative practices. Barbara can be contacted at the Murray Mallee Community Health Service, PO Box 346, Murray Bridge 5253, South Australia.

PART V

Co-research

11

How we learnt that scratching can really be self-abuse:

Co-research with young people[1]

findings presented by[2]

Sharon Nosworthy & Kerry Lane

Preface[3]

Kerry: *The work described in the following paper occurred back in 1994. We were working with young women who were in an accommodation service for homeless young people, and we were concerned about the increase in practices of self-abuse. We were caught in the position of arguing against self-abuse and it really wasn't working. That's when we thought it might be a good idea to seek out some more information.*

Sharon: *We decided that for the first time we would try co-research. I actually think that the main thing that worked was that we admitted that we didn't know what we were doing. We were transparent and were honest with the young people involved and that made an enormous difference. In my experience, we as adults and as professionals are encouraged to present ourselves as being people who know it all. Even if we don't understand the problem, we are encouraged to act as if we know the solutions.*

Kerry: *From what I gather, admitting our confusion and lack of knowledge was a new experience for the young people. I think we managed to communicate that we really wanted their information so we could use it with others and be more helpful. We weren't just trying to find another way to convince them to stop, and that certainly seemed to free us all up.*

There was already a trust relationship to build upon. It was just that we had come to a sticking point about self-abuse. We were trying to come up with ideas and were encouraging them to stop, and in some ways this was turning into an us-against-them thing. I don't think this eroded trust, however, because the young women still knew our motivation was a concern for their safety. They spoke of how having their knowledge valued was a new experience, especially around an issue such as self-abuse. They'd experienced strong negative responses from workers in the past about self-abuse. It was a taboo topic. Usually it wasn't talked about, and when people did talk about it they were often correcting the young people and telling them what to do. The idea of admitting to our lack of knowledge and inviting the young people to share their knowledges was really quite liberating for all of us.

Most of our adult and professional life trains us into believing that we should have the answers. We are encouraged to think that valuable knowledge comes from learning in traditional ways and traditional places as opposed to learning through lived experience. This paper describes the excitement and freedom that we have found in stepping outside of these traditional ways of working.

Introduction

Working with teenagers who self-mutilate[4] raises lots of concerns for the therapist which invite the therapist to take responsibility for safety and argue against self-mutilation. We found ourselves caught in this position with several of the young women we were working with in therapy. Our genuine efforts to be helpful were rejected and met with hostility by the young women, which left us feeling even more scared and useless. We were desperate to find a way to break this vicious cycle. David Epston's ideas on co-research offered us a different position to take. This paper outlines the process used, our concerns, the questions asked, the young women's responses, and the outcome.

Background

We both work with teenagers who are (or are likely to become) homeless, and teenagers who have been sexually abused. In our work we use individual therapy, co-therapy, large and small group work, and personal development camps. Within these different practices we adopt a narrative approach. Two of the young women we were working with were engaging in practices of self-mutilation. By self-mutilation, we mean cutting with knives, razor blades, pieces of glass, mostly on the lower arm and wrist area, occasionally also on the legs. The wounds caused by this mutilation were often serious and required medical attention. Both these young women were mutilating at least weekly. They were living in an accommodation service for young women and were good friends. The mutilation seemed to be escalating and the other residents were beginning to emulate these practices. We attempted to deal with this by arguing for alternatives, by externalizing, by narrative sexual abuse therapy and anything else we thought might be helpful. None of these techniques made any difference to their self-mutilation and in fact seemed to be counter-productive.

We both attended an intensive workshop run by David Epston on the Central Coast. During this workshop David shared his ideas about co-research and how this acknowledges the 'expert knowledge' of the people with whom we work. This gives them an opportunity to pass this knowledge onto us so that our work practices can be more appropriately informed.

We watched a video during the workshop of David doing co-research with a group of young women who had engaged in self-mutilation practices. This group of young women called these practices 'scratching'. We became very excited about these ideas and immediately saw it as something different we could do with the young women we were working with who were also engaging in these practices. We decided to get a group of young women together and co-research scratching.

Some of the concerns we had about conducting this group were:

- *We felt that talking about self-mutilation might become so emotional for everyone that we might not be able to handle the situation.*

- *We were concerned that because there was already a pattern of us arguing against and them arguing for self-mutilation this exercise might become more of the same. If this pattern was reinforced it might encourage more self-mutilation.*

- *We were concerned that we would end up doing 'therapy' rather than 'co-research'.*

- *We were concerned about the reactions of all the workers. As professionals we are trained into the expert role and stepping out of this can be difficult and nerve-racking at first. We were concerned that any of us could slip back into the expert role.*

To address these concerns, we had joint consultation with our professional consultant, Steve Armstrong. Most of our concerns were addressed. The concern that lingered was that our need to achieve therapeutic outcomes for these young women would become the primary focus of the group. In order for this intervention to be different, the focus had to be on gaining access to their 'expert knowledge'. On reflection we realise that prior to the group we were thinking that co-research could not be therapy.

Getting the group together

As this was happening within a residential setting. a group already existed. We also decided to include some ex-residents we had worked with who we knew had engaged in self-mutilation practices and had ceased to do so. We also decided to include the staff of the residential unit as they were also at a loss as to how to handle self-mutilation.

Members of the group

Residents

Karen: Currently severely and regularly self-mutilating

Yvonne: Currently severely and regularly self-mutilating

Katrina: Not self-mutilating but attracted to the idea

Shona: Just started self-mutilating

Melanie: History of self-mutilation not known if current

Ex-residents

Susan: History of self-mutilation not current

Tania: History of self-mutilation not current (as far as we knew)

Workers

Janice: History of self-mutilation not current

Cheryl: History of self-mutilation not current

Cathy: Never self-mutilated

Sharon: Never self-mutilated

Kerry: Never self-mutilated

Setting up the group

The group was held at the accommodation service. We started by explaining our reasons for seeking their co-operation in this research. We explained to them that we had not self-mutilated and therefore had trouble understanding self-mutilation. We also confessed that, despite having tried every therapeutic intervention known to us as well as every conceivable idea that we could come up with between us and in consultation with others, we still felt confused. None of our previous responses to self-mutilation had been helpful. Indeed we were feeling frightened and powerless.

At this point the young women present assured us that we were good counsellors - we just didn't know what we were talking about when it came to self-mutilation. We agreed that we didn't know what we were talking about when it came to self-mutilation and therefore when we had heard about co-research at a recent workshop we had decided to try it. We explained that co-research was not therapy, it was not intended to convince them to stop self-mutilating. The purpose was for them to inform us of what they knew about self-mutilation so that we could be more useful to them and to other young people.[5]

We felt it was of utmost importance to establish safety. In order to do this we developed a set of guidelines. We were open to discussing these so that everybody understood them but they were not negotiable.

- We stated the importance of being respectful of people's opinions and experiences even though they might be different from our own. We told them that we didn't expect that everyone would have the same experience or ideas about self-mutilation.

- We stressed the importance of everybody present maintaining confidentiality. Because of their involvement in therapy and groups these young women were very clear about the meaning of confidentiality and the implications when confidentiality is breached.

- We stressed the importance of people feeling safe in this group and acknowledged that talking about self-mutilation was emotive and that people might feel the need to escape. They agreed that even if they felt like this they would stay in the room as this would be safer for everybody.

- We explained that the staff were not there to supervise them or the process but to participate and to contribute their experiences and opinions in the same way as everyone else.

- We expressed our concern that issues might come up for them after the group had finished. We strongly insisted that those who were willing to participate in the group had to identify an adult person that they could contact within the next 24 hours at any time should they need to. We asked each member of the group, including ourselves, to name their support person and to say how they would contact them. There were two young women who had difficulty identifying someone. We made it clear that the group could not proceed until they had done so, which they did.

Before we began we also sought the approval of the group to use the information that would be generated by the co-research in our ongoing work and to pass it on to others who work with young people. They were more than happy to give it.

The following text shows the questions we asked and the young women's responses in their own words.

Questions and responses

We call it self-mutilation, what do you call it?

'Self-mute', 'self-destruction', 'burning', 'cutting', 'muteing', 'mutilation', 'it'.

They sound like pet names, they don't seem to say what it really is. What is it exactly?

After some discussion the young women decided that if you were to say what it really is you'd have to say it was 'self-abuse'.

If we were working with someone and they started self-abusing, what might be happening for them?

'Violence in the family', 'rape', 'molestation', 'drugs', 'alcohol', 'stress', 'family breakdown', 'others abusing themselves'.

At what times would they be most likely to do it?

'Under pressure', 'no help', 'fighting with parents', 'when they have been drinking'.

What is it? Why might someone choose to do this when they're under pressure?

'It's a stress reliever', 'alternative to suicide', 'turning on yourself', 'anger', 'confusion', 'sadness', 'depression', 'punishment', 'alternative to punishing somebody else', 'blame yourself', 'shield', 'to get attention'.

How do people react when they see signs of self-abuse?

The young women expressed annoyance at people's reactions. They said people were either shocked or said things like, 'You idiot'; 'Either way it puts you further down'; 'They try to talk you out of it like you two do'.

What sort of a relationship do you think young people have with self-abuse?

Most of the group argued that self-abuse was a friend and they felt very strongly about this. They pointed out that it was a friend because it stopped you from hurting others and from killing yourself.

That sounds very noble. Is it a noble friend?

Before the others had a chance to answer, Susan interjected with much passion and said: What kind of a friend would do that to you? It's an enemy!

Susan, did you ever see it as a friend?

Yes.

When did you stop seeing it as a friend and start seeing it as an enemy?

Don't know.

Do you see yourself as having a future without it? Or do you think it will always be with you?[6]

Susan laughed and said: I can just imagine a grandmother when the grandkids want to do something: 'Hang on a minute, I'm just cutting up my arm with my knitting needles' - and she acted this out.

We laughed. Then we became aware that, apart from us and Susan, no-one was laughing.

Do any of you have a problem with us laughing/taking the piss out of it?

No. (but they looked shocked) [7]

Some of the things we do when we're stressed out are self-care things like eating chocolate. Do any of you remember a time when you used self-care?

Blank looks, no response.

We're assuming you didn't always self-abuse - is that a fair assumption? You didn't self-abuse as a baby, did you?

No. (they thought this was funny and made jokes about it) Everyone laughed.

Can you remember what self-care things you used to do?

'Finding someone to call', 'finding someone to listen', 'smoking', 'crying', 'chocolate', 'listen to music', 'shopping', 'other interests', 'sport', 'massage', 'goals', 'spend time with people who don't know your problems', 'exercise', 'have a shower', 'allow yourself to feel', 'create a safe place', 'dancing', 'baths', 'candles', 'hairdressers', 'facial', 'getting a job/achieving', 'yoga/relaxation'.

How does the voice of self-abuse drown out the voice of self-care?

'It just happens', 'you can't predict it', 'you can't stop it', 'you have no control', 'better than killing yourself or hurting others'.

Is there anything that is helpful in making the voice of self-care louder?

No response.

Do we do anything that's helpful?

Yes. (tentative)

What do we do that's helpful?

Being there to talk to.

What do we do that's not helpful?

Karen: *You could be more helpful by not telling people so that they can protect us. (general agreement)*

Sharon: 'My job is to help keep people safe so I have to do something to keep you safe and sometimes that means telling the worker on duty.'

Karen: *That doesn't keep me safe - I'm the only one that can keep me safe.*

Kerry: 'But we have to tell someone - we can't keep quiet about it.'

Karen: *That's okay, tell someone but be honest and say you're doing it because it's abuse, and you can't keep quiet about abuse, not so you can keep us safe, because you can't. (general agreement from the group)*

Okay, thanks for clearing that up. You're absolutely right. I hadn't thought about it like that before.

If you could give someone who was getting into self-abuse advice what would you say to them?

'Don't start it', 'do something else', 'talk about it', 'don't do it', 'don't do it', 'don't do it'.

We'd like to give your advice to the young people we work with - is that okay?

Yes, that's great.

While the above narrative provides the essence of the conversation, it is unable to convey the, at times, highly emotional atmosphere. The group was extremely intense. There were tears and laughter and times when we wondered if our worst fears would be realised. However, after the group finished, we (Kerry and Sharon) both agreed that, rather than feeling worried and burdened by discussing this, we felt a sense of relief and tentative optimism.

Winding up the group

We let the group know that we appreciated their willingness to be honest and to share their knowledge of self-abuse with us. We assured them that we were much clearer about how to be more helpful when working with young people who self-abuse. We asked them how they found the process. They said they felt good about the group and they all agreed that they finally felt that someone had listened to them but then said, 'but it won't stop us from doing it'.

What we learnt from the process

There are many things that we learnt from this process. Our concerns about conducting this group led us to give extensive consideration to how the group should be set up. On reflection we realised that this was an important factor in the success of the co-research process. It meant that we highlighted our lack of knowledge about self-abuse and acknowledged their 'expert knowledge'. We had expressed a genuine interest that stemmed from our need to be helpful. This was acceptable to the young women and addressed their concerns about our motive.

We also learnt the importance of stressing to the young women that the knowledge was gained to assist us in our work with others. This helped them and us to keep the primary focus of the group on gaining access to their 'expert knowledge' rather than achieving therapeutic outcomes. Apart from this influencing our questions, it also influenced their responses and seemed to allow them to be more forthcoming with their knowledge. We realised this because much of the knowledge they shared with us in this group they had not shared with us in any other setting previously.

We feel that the strong emphasis that was placed on establishing safety was essential to the process. It allowed all of us to proceed and it clearly stated our commitment to safety.

We learnt that overall we needed to be careful that the process didn't become therapy-focused rather than co-research focused. We realised this when we looked back on our prepared questions and noted that we had actually prepared some 'therapy' questions but during the group we had automatically changed them to 'co-research' questions. For example, we had prepared the question, 'What's happening for you at the time?' but the question we asked was, 'If we were working with someone and they started self-abusing what might be happening for them?' However, at one point we did slip back into therapy mode. In our excitement in discovering that Susan was articulating views that mirrored our own, we were seduced into encouraging her into expressing her views more fully and asked her, 'When did you stop seeing it as a friend and start seeing it as an enemy?' It was apparent that she was immediately constrained by this personal question and it was clear to us that we had erred.

We felt that it was significant that the young women reached consensus on the name 'self-abuse' early in the process, as this had an impact on the questions we asked and the tone of the co-research. This group considered the term 'self-abuse' most appropriate. Our very strong 'anti-abuse' stand with these young women no doubt influenced their language and made it much more likely that they would name 'abuse' when they recognised it. Other groups may consider other descriptions more appropriate. We were committed to proceed with whatever description they came up with.

The staff participated in the same way as the young women and feedback from them was very positive. As workers we mostly managed to stay out of the expert role.

Conclusion

This group was held in mid-1994. Since then we have used the knowledge gained from the group in our therapy with these young women and with others. Most of the young people we have shared this knowledge with have readily accepted the description of self-mutilation as 'self-abuse'. It appears that when the young people embrace this new description they are much more likely to reject the practices of 'self-abuse'.

The lifestyles of these young women remain much the same. Difficult times have arisen, times when they would normally have turned to self-abuse for relief, but instead they have used some of the 'self-care' ideas they came up with in the group. To our surprise only one of these young women has engaged in self-abuse in the eight months since the group was held in mid-1994. She faced a series of traumatic events and reports that after trying 'self-care' she eventually resorted to 'self-abuse' when things continued to escalate. This young woman also stated that she returned to 'self-abuse' only this once and is now becoming much more familiar and accepting of 'self-care'. Despite this one come-back by 'self-abuse' we are not disheartened. It should be remembered that 'self-abuse' was a dominant force in the lives of these young women, one that some of them resorted to weekly.

After being introduced to the idea of co-research, we felt certain that we would gain a lot of knowledge from these young women, however we were not sure what the benefit might be for them. We are therefore thrilled with the therapeutic outcomes for these young women and are confident that this experience will allow us to work in a more helpful way with other young people. We have decided that there is definitely an opportunity for our work to be informed by co-research in the future on this and other topics.

This is how we learnt that, for this specific group of young women, 'Scratching is really self-abuse'.

Notes

1. First published in the 1996 No.4 issue of the *Dulwich Centre Newsletter*. Republished here with permission.

2. Kerry has worked for seven years in the field of family therapy with children, young people and families on the central coast of New South Wales, Australia. She has worked as a family counsellor with families with young children considered to be 'at risk'; as an adolescent and family counsellor with homeless or potentially homeless adolescents and their families; as a child and adolescent sexual assault counsellor; and is currently employed as an adolescent counsellor with young people who sexually abuse. Sharon has worked for eight years as an adolescent and family counsellor with homeless or potentially homeless adolescents and their families.

   Sharon and Kerry work in a narrative way with individuals, families and large groups. Their work together includes: therapeutic weekends with large groups of teenagers; protective behaviour groups for teenagers; and co-research projects with teenagers. They can be contacted c/- PO Box 292, Bay Village NSW 2261, Australia.

3. The preface and postscript to this paper were created from an interview with Sharon and Kerry that took place in May 1996 with Taruna Mclean.

4. We recognise that the term 'self-mutilation' might be regarded as having judgemental overtones. However, it is used in this paper simply to refer to a range of self-injurious practices. Also, the young women themselves used this and similar terms.

   We would be keen to hear from readers about their thoughts on this topic. Please write to us c/- PO Box 292, Bay Village NSW 2261, Australia.

5. In retrospect, we acknowledge that we did not voice our hope that there would be positive individual outcomes for the young women. It was not our intention to mislead the young women. In fact we had not even voiced these hopes to each other.

6. Although the previous two questions had been directed to Susan, this question was not. It was a general question directed to the group.

7. The atmosphere at this point was very tense. We realised that, in laughing at self-abuse, we had highlighted our lack of regard for it. This lack of regard appeared to horrify the group and we quickly moved on.

Postscript

Kerry: *The process of co-research has been absolutely liberating. I don't feel like I have to have all the answers or that people even want me to. It has made my work easier, because once we have actually discussed some of these things with some young people, then I can come to another young person and say, 'When I was talking to other young people they have said this, this, this, this, and this. Do any of those things fit for you?' It has given me information for working with young people who may not be able to be so open and vocal about those topics. They have the opportunity to say, 'That's right, that is how I feel', or 'It's a bit like that but ...' It just opens the whole thing up. Also, one big learning has been about safety. Originally I genuinely believed that I could keep young people safe if I tried really hard, and did everything that was humanly possible. I realise now that I can't.*

Sharon: *It doesn't matter how much effort you put in, you cannot keep them safe.*

Kerry: *That's right, so I guess that has really made a difference. I haven't felt defeated by it.*

Sharon: *That has made a big difference and now I don't feel as responsible when I have clients who are making unsafe decisions. I still worry and still care but I don't feel as responsible.*

Kerry: *Yes, it does feel different and I'm sure it feels different for them too. It's like an acknowledgment of their ability to deal with difficult situations, which cause them to make decisions around their own safety. So I think that has been a major thing that I have learnt that has really influenced my approach to my work. I guess one of the things that the process of co-research has enabled has been to give us some language to use and some ideas to go on with. I now feel very comfortable in talking about self-abuse with young people, and exploring their attitudes to it.*

I have also come to see that co-research, far from being separate from therapy, is actually therapeutic in itself. For a young person to be asked their opinions and to have them valued is part of the therapeutic process.

Sharon: *Now that I have become involved in co-research I find I can't keep the two things separate. Even if I am working with one young person and I am in* the counselling room, I find myself asking co-research questions - it seems to seep into my mind. Co-research to me doesn't mean asking curious questions when I already have a set idea of the answer, it involves genuinely seeking young people's opinions and knowledges.

Once you start it creates ripples. It was once a really strong belief around here that every time a young person self-harms or self-abuses they are practicing suicide. I don't know where this view comes from. I think we must be trained into those sorts of beliefs. Co-research and consulting young people about their alternative realities can challenge our training. It also encourages us to think of alternative ways of working. Working so close to life and death can be overwhelming if you are feeling responsible for other people's lives. It is very easy to be invited into arguing against self-abuse. At times of absolute desperation I have known workers to fall back into threatening punishment. We as workers need support in these areas and good conversations. I feel that through the co-research we have been offered a whole repertoire, a whole language that has come from the young people that is an alternative view, that doesn't invite us into arguing, let alone punitive responses. That has been liberating for us.

12

Caucusing as communication[1]

by[2]

Sharon Nosworthy & Kerry Lane

The caucusing process

Co-research is an attempt to work in ways that honour the experiences and knowledges of young people and enable adult workers to step outside of expert roles (see 'How we learnt that scratching can really be self-abuse' in this newsletter). During camps on the central coast of New South Wales we have been exploring co-research involving young people and workers which incorporates caucusing and reflecting team work. These camps involve young people, aged fourteen to eighteen years old, and the counsellors with whom the young people have been working. The camps offer the possibility to develop different sorts of relationships between workers and young people and aim to enrich the ongoing counselling relationships.

The caucusing process begins with the workers asking a series of questions to young people around a particular theme, for example what they find most and least helpful about the counselling process. The young people split up into small groups to consider the questions. The groups do not contain an adult and instead are made up of young people with differing levels of experience in caucusing. These groups then report back to the large group. The workers sit outside the large circle of young people and listen to their discussions about the questions and each group's responses. The workers then sit in the middle of the room with the young people in a large circle around them. They reflect on the information they have received. They may seek clarification or expansion on what the young people have reported. The workers' responses are not designed to come from an expert position but instead to reflect on how the information that they have heard, and the process itself, may affect the ways they will work in future (see White 1995 for a detailed description of the role and purposes of reflecting teams).

The workers then join the large circle and a general discussion about the process is held. The young people have the opportunity to give feedback to the workers' reflecting team, about how they experienced the reflections, and about any other issues that have been raised by the discussion.

The following questions and answers are the result of a co-research caucusing process that took place at a camp in March 1996. The questions were asked by the workers, and each group response represents a caucus of young people.

What things do young people do that you find supportive?

Group 1:   *Understand where you are coming from; you can always rely on good, close friends; give you cigarettes.*

Group 2:   *To be able to respect; not backstabbing; not bitching; believing what you tell them; telling the truth, not lying; keeping confidential; not putting you down; letting you be yourself.*

Group 3:   *Being there for you; sharing experiences; shoulders to cry on; love; support; trust; hugs; listening.*

Group 4:   *Share their problems; listen to you; give hugs; supportive; they treat you like an equal; like a friend; they care.*

What things do counsellors do that you find supportive?

Group 1: *Stand by you; listen to what you say; try to understand you; help you when no-one else will; respect confidentiality.*

Group 2: *Talking; ringing you back when you ring them; understanding what you want out of that relationship; believing you and giving you trust; confidentiality; being supportive in legal matters.*

Group 3: *Listen; they don't judge you; give advice; help; care; sharing own experiences; not expecting too much; go out of their way to help; loving; confidential.*

Group 4: *When they are worried they care about you; when they talk about themselves; when they hug you; take you out to places; when they try to understand you; when they invite you to camp; when they treat you as a mate.*

Young people's experience of caucusing

Kristy, Kylie, Leanne and Ryan have participated as young people in a number of these caucusing processes. In the interview below they speak about their experiences of the co-research caucusing process:[3]

Kristy: *It's good to have adults ask questions and then actually listen to what you have decided to say. It helps clear the air and also there is a chance for them to hear what would make things better.*

Leanne: *It's a good way of doing it because we are a bigger force when we are a group. When you are an individual you are only a small force but when you ...*

Ryan: *It's like you are holding hands and can knock anything over!*

Kristy: *It is good because what you have come up with, what you have thought about, the solutions you have come up with, are going to help other people, and that's great.*

Kylie: *It makes us feel like equals. At school we always have to get our parents' permission for everything. If you are sick you have to get your parents' permission before you can go home. You are not treated on equal basis. The camps are different in that it becomes a two-way street. We're not the only ones who have to spill the beans. The most special part is when the workers go around and talk about their reactions. We are always quiet then, because we like to hear what they have to say. At first we thought they'd say things like what they thought needed to be done, but it was different. We were all in it together and they just talked about their views and what it had meant to them to listen to us.*

Leanne: *I agree. The best part of the caucus is when the adults get in the middle and talk about their responses. Usually when we speak adults go away into a room and all sit down and stay in there all talking about it. We're left out there thinking, 'What are they saying and what are they thinking?' But this way we can see how everyone has interpreted what we have said. We can see if they've got it straight, and if they haven't we can set them straight. Otherwise when workers go away into a room we 'um and ah' and are left wondering. It is good to hear what they have to say.*

Ryan: *The format of the camp and other stuff has changed due to these sessions. We can talk stuff through in small groups. It would be so much harder as one big group.*

Kristy: *It's hard to imagine this sort of thing happening in schools. I can only think of one or two teachers who would want to try it. But that's something, I guess.*

Ryan: *A lot of the kids would probably think it's weird too.*

Kylie: *I think it would be great if it did happen in schools. It would make kids want to go to school a lot more. If you went there and it was more like the camps where you had the caucusing, it would work a lot better. You'd feel like going.*

Leanne: *The most important thing is for workers to just listen.*

Kristy: *And to believe us. Usually if you say something like, 'I reckon an adult has done something wrong', then all the adults say, 'No, you are lying'. They gang up. It is the same with teachers. You cannot get a teacher in trouble unless you can prove it. But on the camps people will listen first and then try to find a solution.*

Ryan: *With the caucusing, when something is being done that we don't like, we can say stuff as a group and it gets addressed. It helps us to be listened to and then we all look at the situation.*

Kylie: *We've done it before when workers do things that aren't okay. We go up and say we think so-and-so has done this wrong. Then we all sit down and discuss it and sort it out.*

Ryan: *I wish that happened in schools rather than it being they're right and you're wrong.*

Kristy: *Yeah, usually adults don't get to know you first. They just assume that this is what you have done and this is what you are going to be like for the rest of your life. They stereotype us.*

Kylie: *Lots of workers are too professional, you can't get close enough to them. You can talk about everyday life, sort of thing, and they don't judge you, but then they won't comment like on how you were at a funeral or something - the important stuff.*

Kristy: *I like it when it feels we are doing things together. Normally when adults and young people are in the same place the adults usually want to stay separate. But at the camps we are all equal, kind of. We are all together.*

To hear young people, in caucusing sessions, describe what they find helpful from both workers and young people has been a powerful experience for us. It has put us in touch with our own stories about being young and what helped us through difficult times. It has invited us to consider both the strengths and restraints of friendship for young people in our culture. Importantly, as workers, we have often been surprised by young people's responses. When they have spoken about what they value in counselling relationships, it has become clear that it isn't expert knowledge or our professional techniques that are of most value, but instead simple displays of caring and the building of solid, trusting relationships. In other sessions, the importance of the camps and the importance of seeing counsellors in different settings have been articulated. Young people have let us know that having the opportunity to relate to counsellors outside of counselling sessions, where counsellors are seen in a different light, has been enriching of the relationships.

The caucusing process is an invigorating one for us. It is also an experience of sharing and communication that is rare in our culture. The structures seem to enable collective conversations. They provide us with both information and encouragement and build upon our relationships - both between young people and counsellors and between counsellors. The caucusing also in some way provides a sense of security, a sense that there is a process for feedback that can help keep us on track. It is an ongoing process and we are continually learning how the ways in which we work are either replicating adults' power over young people, or are building alternative ways of working and being. As a result of requests from young people, it has been decided that at future camps we as workers will be asked questions that have been developed by the young people. The process which we described above will be reversed. We look forward to ongoing changes in the process as we see this as simply a starting point in trying to develop structures that will enable meaningful communication across generations.

Notes

1. First published in the 1996 No.4 issue of the *Dulwich Centre Newsletter.* Republished here with permission.

2. Kerry has worked for seven years in the field of family therapy with children, young people and families on the central coast of New South Wales, Australia. She has worked as a family counsellor with families with young children considered to be 'at risk'; as an adolescent and family counsellor with homeless or potentially homeless adolescents and their families; as a child and adolescent sexual assault counsellor; and is currently employed as an adolescent counsellor with young people who sexually abuse. Sharon has worked for eight years as an adolescent and family counsellor with homeless or potentially homeless adolescents and their families.

   Sharon and Kerry work in a narrative way with individuals, families and large groups. Their work together includes: therapeutic weekends with large groups of teenagers; protective behaviour groups for teenagers; and co-research projects with teenagers. They can be contacted c/- PO Box 292, Bay Village NSW 2261, Australia.

3. This interview took place on the 21st May 1996 in Gosford, New South Wales with Taruna McLean, Sharon Nosworthy and Kerry Lane. Kristy, Kylie, Leanne and Ryan have chosen not to include their second names.

Reference

White, M. 1995: 'Reflecting teamwork as definitional ceremony.' In White, M., *Re-Authoring Lives: Interviews and Essays*. Adelaide: Dulwich Centre Publications.

PART VI

Power to
our
Journeys

13

Power to Our Journeys[1]

by[2]

Brigitte, Sue, Mem, and Veronika

We would like to introduce ourselves as members of the Power to Our Journeys group based at Dulwich Centre in Adelaide, Australia. We would like you to know that all of us have been recipients of mainstream psychiatric services for varying lengths of time, have had admissions to psychiatric hospitals, have been subject to various treatments, and have all been assigned various diagnoses over this time. The people who have treated us have mostly settled on the diagnosis of schizophrenia.

How did we get together? It was our experiences of narrative therapy that provided the basis for our connection with each other. Through this therapy we had the opportunity to change our relationship with the voices and with the visions that were troubling to us and traumatising of us. This opened space for us to break from the prison house of isolation and to join in new connections with others who are engaged in similar projects to reclaim their lives.

We get together as a group once per month and invite Michael White to join us to keep a special record of our conversation and to ask questions that assist us to express our thoughts on various issues. After each of these meetings he puts together our ideas in a document which serves as a record of our evolving knowledges and of the development in our skills of living. These documents are a powerful resource to us in our work to recover our lives and in assisting us to deal with crises. We have included three examples of these documents here in the hope they will be of assistance to others.

Our reason for joining in the writing of this piece is to share with you the extent to which our lives have changed through our involvement in the Power to Our Journeys group. This group has played a very significant part in rekindling our love for life, and in assisting us to achieve a quality of life we could never have predicted. It is our hope that others who are struggling with troublesome voices and visions will find hope in what we have to say here, and join us in spirit by searching for others they might connect with in similar ways.

Acknowledgement of our experience

The Power to Our Journeys meetings provide a forum for us to talk about many of our experiences of life. This includes our experiences of what others refer to as auditory or visual hallucinations, or, if you like, the psychoses. It is our preference to refer to these experiences as ones of 'voices' and 'visions'.

Over the many years of our different connections with psychiatric services, we have found little opportunity to speak openly of our day-to-day experiences of the voices and visions that have been so troublesome to us, or, for that matter, the voices and visions that have been helpful to our lives. We have been silenced time and again by many psychiatric professionals who have consistently refused to acknowledge our experiences of these voices and visions. At times we have been bewildered by this, at a loss to understand it. At times we have linked this silencing to the fear we see in the eyes of others. Perhaps they experience this fear because we put them in touch with how vulnerable they might be in their own struggles in life, and with a realisation of how thin the line is between where they stand in life and where we stand in life. At other times we understand others believe that to make space for us to talk more openly about our experiences of troublesome voices and visions is counterproductive. We know that still others are caught up in weird theories about our experiences, and talk about our lives in ways that subtract from our sense of self-respect and make it impossible for them to hear what we have to say about our experiences of voices and visions. And we meet others who are so caught up in professional career and institutional considerations of a hierarchical nature that it is impossible for them to be with us in healing ways.

Needless to say, this silencing has profoundly negative consequences for all of our lives. All of us have felt abandoned because of this. We have not felt joined with by others at those times in our lives when this was what we have longed for most. At times this very silencing has contributed to a sense that we might be going mad. And it has made it virtually impossible for us to change our relationship with the troublesome voices and visions that have been so dominating of our lives, and, as well, with the voices and visions that have been more supportive of us.

Changing our relationship with the voices

We cannot here emphasise strongly enough how important it is to have the opportunity to speak of the troublesome voices and visions in a forum that contributes to a powerful exposé of their purposes and their operations. These troublesome voices and visions can be quite vicious, and from time to time give us an incredibly hard time. They have at their disposal many well-established tactics for tyrannising our lives: to frighten us, to get us into a panic, and to drive us to desperation. In developing an exposé of the purposes and operations of these voices and visions, we become clearer about the extent to which what they want for our lives is not in our interests, and we become increasingly knowledgable about the strategies they utilise to achieve their purposes. This exposé disempowers them, and opens up possibilities for us to become much more aware of the knowledges and skills we have that we can put to work to frustrate the attempts of the voices and visions to capture our lives. By meeting together to extend this exposé and to further pool our knowledges and skills, we have all been able to further change our relationships with the troublesome voices and visions so they become less dominant in our lives.

This has not been achieved without work. As we have extended these exposés, we have put more effort into monitoring the activities of the troublesome voices and visions, and, as well, into the monitoring of our general sense of well-being. Doing this is a commitment we have made to ourselves and to each other, and it has opened new possibilities in our lives. For example, we know that we are more vulnerable to the more troublesome voices and visions when we are stressed out or stretched, and we can make predictions about those occasions and conditions upon which these voices and visions might attempt to get the upper hand in our lives. We can also make predictions about the sort of tactics they might resort to in these attempts. Then, as we prepare to take new steps in our lives, or to venture into unfamiliar territory, we can refer to this knowledge. This provides us with the opportunity to put things in place that will support us through these changes, and to prepare countertactics to have at the ready should the voices and visions attempt to harass us. We are then more able to recognise such attempts for what they are, to step back and say to ourselves 'So, that is what you are up to', and then take the sort of action that will deprive them of these moments as an opportunity to strengthen their influence in our lives. The knowledge that we have options at these times provides an antidote to the insecurity that the troublesome voices and visions feed on.

The negative voices and visions are wreckers

So that you might understand more fully how important it has been for us to find a space in which we can talk of our experiences of the troublesome voices and visions and to put together these exposés, you should know what 'wreckers' these voices and visions can be. Jobs, friends, interests, hopes, status - these voices and visions took so much, and tried to ruin what they couldn't take. We grieved for the losses. Our families grieved for themselves and for us over the loss of the potential that we would never fulfil. It is not that others didn't support us. They tried to help. But there was a limit to what they could do. Many of our relatives became frightened and despairing. We lost friends to exhaustion and to terror. Some of us became homeless for years, just going from place to place.

There were friends and relatives who managed to hang in, but we didn't know how to help them understand or to know what to do. And, even if we had, we would not have been able to act on this knowledge as we had our hands full just trying to stay alive. As we began to realise what a burden we were becoming, we retreated. We just went away. We 'went bush', or were even alone in the company of others. This was all we could do to protect our relatives and friends from the trauma. And, in the end, this isolation served the interests of the troublesome voices and visions, not our interests.

Lightness of being

But we grieve no longer. We have found that a lot of the grief was about the loss of a status we no longer have a desire for, and that, in fact, we are glad to be free of. And now we are finding the opportunity to talk openly with friends and relatives about the pain they experienced in relation to what we went through during the hard times. Although it is true that some friendships died, those that didn't have been renewed and enriched by these conversations.

Our experiences of our own lives have changed significantly, and this is accompanied by a different happiness, a happiness that has to do with how we approach the smaller things of life. We are more able to appreciate our own thoughts, and find that we have a sense of living well when we are able to get out of bed in the morning and when we are able to catch a bus or a tram. We are experiencing more just about being in the flow of life. We know more about what makes some places healing places to be in.

It is not that we still don't have hard times. We do. But, in revising our relationships with the troublesome voices and visions, and through our work together in the Power to Our Journeys group, we have also stepped into an experience of life we could never have predicted. We know it probably sounds strange, but we have achieved a quality of life, a richness, when living with the voices that would be difficult for many to understand. This has to do with many things, including a shift in what we value. For example, we have all experienced a change in our position on traditional materialistic values. It is not that we have dispensed with all materialistic values, it is just that they no longer mean what they meant to us previously. These values are no longer the elevated values. They have a different place in our lives. This means that many of our old associations with happiness no longer mean much to us. Instead, it is the lightness of being that we experience from moment to moment that matters most to us. And it is the mischievousness that we find becoming more and more a part of our every-day sense of our lives, of our humour, that is important. We even are able to embrace the fact that, in many ways, we stand outside of what is expected of people in our culture, and to poke fun at these expectations. At these times we feel like larrikins, and the feeling is just great. All this means that on those occasions when we feel at risk of again being caught up in a tempest, we don't quite lose sight of the sun.

Our membership of the Power to Our Journeys group has contributed very significantly to this lightness of being. We are together in solidarity. We are secure in each other's company, knowing we have coped with lots of changes in our lives, and that we have gained knowledge through successfully managing the difficulties we have experienced at these times. We confirm this with each other at those times when we are vulnerable to the troublesome voices and visions, and become firm in the understanding that this has to do with facing the next step in life. We have learned how to be there for each other outside of our formal meeting times, supporting each other through difficult challenges. We have learned how to help each other stay in touch with the powerful knowledges we have developed together. And we have found that the troublesome voices and visions are allergic to this sort of team work.

Justice

It has been important for us to experience our work to reclaim our lives from the troublesome voices and visions as a struggle against injustice. These voices and visions are oppressive, and since our work on revising our relationship with these voices and visions addresses issues of power and control, then this relationship is a political relationship. This political understanding provides us with strength, as it keeps us in touch with the fact that we are not just on a personal journey, but also on a political journey.

It would be true to say that our work together has rekindled not just a love for life, but a love for justice, and this sustains us in our lives. This commitment to justice reinforced our decision to put this piece together. It also reinforces our claim to friendship, to love, to security, and to understanding. As we explore together notions of justice, we develop greater clarity about the fact that we do not have to put up with our lives being spoken about in ways that reduce us, in pathologising and marginalising ways. And we become more effective in our challenges to these ways of speaking about our lives and the lives of others who experience troublesome voices and visions.

Medication

We have all had a variety of experiences with medication, some of these satisfactory, some of them not. It is clear to us all that our experiences with medications become more satisfactory when we consider them to be tools for us, not ends in themselves. Drugs are tools that open space for us to work with others on the exposé of the troublesome voices and visions, on our friendships, and in the honouring of our knowledge of life. It is in this space that we can get our heads together. So, drugs can open up possibilities for us to take action to free ourselves from domination. However, it is of critical importance that we don't allow drugs to oppress us. We use drugs, but won't be used by them.

Logo

The Power to Our Journeys group has a logo. It is of Mount Kilimanjaro. Quite some years ago, Sue, one of the members of our group, climbed to the top of this mountain. In one of our meetings she remarked that getting her life back from the hostile voices was a journey that was not dissimilar to the climb to the top of Mount Kilimanjaro. 'It is hard work', she said, 'but with the right preparations and provisions, a good map of the terrain, access to forecasts that make it possible to predict the weather ahead, and the appropriate support systems, it can be done.' We all embrace this philosophy. We will continue to equip ourselves with these tools and to develop the sort of support systems that will make it possible for us to see this journey through.

Conclusion

It has been proposed elsewhere that the libraries of psychiatric hospitals be obliged to include the sort of alternative texts that might be created by collections of the sort of therapeutic documents that we provide examples of here, and that these be placed alongside the more formal psychiatric texts. These alternative texts just might be more helpful to people who are struggling with troublesome voices and visions than the standard texts. We hope this is true, and that we have been able to contribute to such a possibility in some small way by putting this piece together. This piece doesn't say all we would like to share with you, but we think it will be enough for you to get some understanding of what the Power to Our Journeys group is all about, and for you to get a sense of the spirit in which we undertake our journeys. Because of considerations of space, we haven't here discussed the work we do to revise our relationship with the more supportive voices and visions so that we feel less alone or less abandoned, and more sustained, during hard times. Perhaps we could share this with you at another time.

As authors, we have chosen to identify ourselves by our first names only. This is mainly because stigma is still alive and well in our communities, and we already have enough of this to deal with in our daily lives.

We would like to acknowledge the contribution of those members of the Power to Our Journeys group who did not wish to join the collective that put this piece together. Their voices are echoed in what we have written here. We would like to thank family and friends for persisting in their support of us despite their discouragement, and the workers of the Community Mental Health Project for walking beside us in our steps to achieve what we want for our lives. If you have responses to this piece that you would like to share with us, please send them to us at the address below. However, because we are generally quite busy with the priorities we have shared with you here, we cannot undertake to answer all correspondence.

Notes

1. This piece was first published in the Summer 1996 edition of the American Family Therapy Association *(AFTA) Newsletter*, and was republished with permission in the 1997 No.1 issue of the *Dulwich Centre Newsletter* (also republished here with permission).

2. Brigitte, Sue, Mem and Veronika collectively authored this article, incorporating in it the voices and spirits of the other members of the Power to Our Journeys group. With fellow Power to Our Journeys members, they composed the documentary statements accompanying this article. The authors can be contacted c/- Power to Our Journeys, Dulwich Centre, 345 Carrington Street, Adelaide 5000, South Australia.

Power to Our Journeys

a song by
Sue & David
(copyright 1995)

Verse 1

A journey of 1,000 miles begins with one step
We're coming together now, we're talking 'bout respect
It shouldn't be too much to ask to listen and to learn
To fill the libraries with strategies that work

Chorus: There is power to our journey
There is hope in this room
Voices to be heard
And stories to be told
(repeat chorus)

Verse 2

What could this be that we've planted here today?
What could this be that we are watering so carefully?
Could they be friendships, something so sacred, yet so simple?
Could they be friend 'ships' to sail?
(chorus and repeat chorus)

Verse 3

As we tell our stories, we remember friends on similar journeys
We take their hands, and join them in rage
And join them in sorrow, and join them in hopefulness
(chorus and repeat chorus)

Verse 4

Well, we're trying to get it together
But, together we have it all
Well, we're trying to get it together
But, together we have it all
We are silently boiling over, we are silently boiling over
We are silently boiling over, we are silently boiling over
(chorus and repeat chorus)

Last line

There is power to our journey.

Document 1

Solidarity

1. We first talked about the techniques that the troublesome voices resort to in their attempts to get the upper hand in our lives. It was interesting that we all had similar observations to make about these techniques and all understood how important it was to expose them. The voices resort to these techniques as they engage in those undesirable activities that are against our interests.

2. The techniques that were exposed during the meeting fell into different categories, all of which relate to certain characteristics of the voices:
   a. It was established that the voices are parasites. They feed off guilt, insecurity, and fear.
   b. It was determined that the voices are opportunists. They take advantage of people when they are stressed-out and feeling vulnerable.
   c. It was determined that the voices are sensationalists. They have the habit of blowing things way out of proportion and, in so doing, of provoking our anxiety.
   d. It was established that the voices are dependent. They rely for their survival upon self-neglect and self-accusations.

3. It was generally understood that to expose the techniques of the voices in this way is of great importance because it makes visible the voices' Achilles' heel. For example, the voices' allergies become rather obvious:
   a. They just cannot stand self-love and self-acceptance.
   b. Self-care throws them into a real fit.
   c. Self-respect is toxic to them.
   d. They are simply terrified of the possibilities of people uniting together in solidarity against them.
   e. Challenging the sensationalism with the facts totally undermines their foundations.
   f. Reclaiming personal power repels their efforts to feed on guilt and fear.

4. Apart from all of this, the voices are also allergic to seeing things clearly. We all agreed that the idea of 'love as a movement through life' is one that assists in establishing an immunity to the voices' techniques.

5. This document is a declaration of solidarity. It is a declaration of the fact that the members of the Power to Our Journeys group are uniting and standing together against the forces that have attempted to tyrannise our lives. This is a way of giving notice to the voices, which, try as they might, will not, in the end, succeed in their attempts to capture our lives. We will carry with us the spirit of this group as we walk through life, and at those times when we are stretched and most vulnerable to being hassled by the voices, we will recreate the experience of this solidarity. This will provide for us a great deal of security and comfort in the face of adversity.

Document 2

Our Determination

1. Mentioning the Unmentionable

We are committed to mentioning the unmentionable, and acknowledge the courage and strength this requires of us. Our achievements in mentioning the unmentionable undermine our guilt, fear, panic and self-doubt. It is also a service to others in that it brings relief to them. It helps others break free from restricting stereotypes.

2. Doing Things at Our Own Pace

We are determined to proceed in life at a pace that suits us, and not at a pace that suits the voices. The voices can be counted upon to push us into doing things before we are ready, and if they succeed, then our minds get clogged up and we lose sight of how we want to be in life. The voices at times rely upon outside support in their attempts to push us into things, and at times this support is unwittingly given by people like rehabilitation officers.

3. Acknowledging Our Teamwork

We are determined to keep sight of the fact that we are members of a team that is the size and as strong as the ocean, and as intelligent as the dolphins. Regardless of the exertions that some others engage in over their attempts to elevate this authority over our lives, we will stay in touch with the strength, the intelligence, and the beauty of our teamwork. Staying in touch with this is effective in shutting the voices up.

4. Honouring the Little Steps

We are committed to the honouring of the so-called 'little steps' we take in life. These are the kinds of steps that so many people in this world overlook, and they include getting out of bed, having a shower, and caring for our lives in general. We will not allow this culture's overriding concern with control to take away our appreciation of these little sacraments of daily life. Instead, we will take pride in them, and in the process, take note of our specialness.

Document 3

Authors of Our Own Lives

1. We are becoming more skilled at identifying our troublesome voices. The more we do this, the clearer it becomes that we are hearing certain voices of society that express some of the dominant attitudes around today.

2. We are developing the ability to stand back from the voices. This helps us to stop evaluating ourselves so much, and makes it possible for us to focus on and to analyse the harassing voices. When we do this, we get to understand just how much these voices have difficulty coping with our movements through our present and into our futures.

3. Knowing that these evaluative, and at times hostile, voices are insecurities is an important realisation. It puts us in touch with the fact that they do not like change, and that it is their wish that we restrict our lives to their home territory.

4. We understand why they try to make us panic when we take up the adventures of life. We also understand why they try to obscure the skills and knowledges we have to bring to our journeys in life. When we openly acknowledge these skills, the voices can get desperate.

5. We can see that the voices are now losing ground and we look forward to the time when they lose any hope of regaining it. They are aware of the fact that the ripples of our work are going out. They are aware of the extent to which the lives of people in other parts of the world are being touched by our lives, and being enriched by the knowledges we are sharing with each other.

6. It appears that the voices have no answer to the creation of these networks. This means a lot. As we journey together in this work, we are becoming better focused, more able to get our feet firmly on the ground in regaining control over our lives, and we are experiencing the personal dignity that is our entitlement.

7. These kinds of developments are freeing of us, and make it easier for us to put other peoples' authority over our lives to one side. It also makes it easier for us to consult ourselves about our own lives and about the kinds of steps that would be nurturing of ourselves. In this way, we are having more to say about our own identities. We are becoming more the authors of our own lives.

PART VII

Some notes

by

Michael White

These notes have been gathered together from various sources. 'Notes on externalizing problems' was first published in the 1996 No.3 issue of the *Dulwich Centre Newsletter*. 'Notes on narrative metaphor and narrative therapy' and 'Notes on power and the culture of therapy' have been extracted from some of Michael's workshop handouts.

Notes on
externalizing problems

The concept of 'externalizing problems' was introduced to the field of family therapy by Michael White (see White & Epston 1990). It is a way of viewing problems and the ways in which people relate to them.

Within our culture there are many invitations for people who have experienced difficult circumstances to see themselves as the problem, as deficient in some way. This can result in people feeling helpless to take any action, or can restrict them to action that reinforces the problem. If you see yourself as the problem there's not much you can do except maybe act against yourself. There are also many invitations to blame relationships for the negative effects of problems. When this occurs people often feel divided from each other at precisely the times that those relationships are most needed.[1]

Externalizing practices involve a refusal to see problems as within people or as within relationships. The person is not the problem, the problem is the problem. 'Externalizing conversations' are conversations that create space for people to see themselves as separate from the problems that are affecting their lives. Once a problem is seen as separate from the identity of a person or from the identity of a significant relationship, the person is in a position to take new action. S/he has the opportunity to resist or protest the problem, and/or renegotiate their relationship with the problem in other ways.

There can be many different types of externalizing conversations. Those engaged in life-threatening problems where the problem has no redeeming features may have the aim of dispelling the problem from their lives. Other externalizing conversations with less threatening problems may emphasise possibilities for a revision of the person's relationship with the problem. Yet other externalizing conversations may not necessarily be with problems *per se*, but take up issues or themes in a way that it becomes possible for people to think differently about aspects of their lives.

One way of externalizing the problem to assist people in uniting together has been to personify the problem. In these circumstances, problems are given an identity and people are invited to consider their relationships with the problem and how these might be altered. An example of this version is the 'Externalizing conversations exercise' originally proposed by Sallyann Roth and David Epston (1998) and revised by Michael White (in McLean 1995, pp.57-59) which is reprinted below.

Externalizing conversations exercise

This exercise has been developed to assist people to explore externalizing conversations. It requires the participation of three or more people. One person volunteers to role-play a problem, another to role-play the person who is experiencing the problem (in this exercise, this person is called the problem's 'subject', and it can be the person who is considered to have the actual problem), and the third to role-play an investigative reporter (a detective-type journalist who is good at exposing subterfuge and corruption). If there are more than three people joining the exercise, there can be more than one investigative reporter, or there can be observers who share their reflections on the exercise at the end.

There are three parts to the exercise. In the first part, the person who is playing the investigative reporter interviews the person who is playing the problem about the problem's successes. In the second part, the person who is playing the investigative reporter interviews the person who is playing the problem about the problem's failures. During these parts of the exercise, the person who is role-playing the subject listens carefully without interrupting. In the third part of the exercise, the person who is playing the subject will have the opportunity to share, with the other players, their experiences of these two interviews.

Part one

After a decision has been made about the problem to be played, and after roles have been assigned, the person who is playing the problem is informed that problems tend to be rather arrogant and boastful, and that it is rarely difficult to get them to talk about their successes and to 'spill the beans' on how they have achieved these successes. In fact, they are so 'full of themselves' that they usually give away their secrets and bring themselves undone as soon as they are given even the slightest opportunity to do so. For this reason, the person who is playing the problem will find themselves in quite a co-operative mood during the interview with the investigative reporter.

It is important that the investigative reporter stay on track with their task. It is not their job to cure the problem, or in any way to attempt to reform it or to rehabilitate it. Instead they should assume the position from which they might simply develop an exposé on the life and the identity of the problem. This is sometimes difficult for the person who is playing the investigative reporter to achieve, and requires some conscious effort to break from the tendency of wanting to be helpful.

The investigative reporter has many options for questions in the development of an exposé on the problem's successes. These questions can open inquiry into:

a) the problem's influence in the different areas of the subject's life (for example, its effects on the subject's relationship with others, its impact on the subject's feelings, its interference in the subject's thoughts, its effects on the subject's story about who they are as a person, how it has the subject treating their own life, and so on);

b) the strategies, the techniques, the deceits, and the tricks that the problem has resorted to in its efforts to get the upper-hand in the subject's life;

c) the special qualities possessed by the problem that it depends upon to undermine and to disqualify the subject's knowledges and skills. This can include an inquiry into the powerful ways that the problem speaks in its efforts to impose its authority on the subject's life;

d) the purposes that guide the problem's attempts to dominate the subject's life, and the dreams and hopes that the problem has for the subject's life;

e) who stands with the problem, and an investigation into the various forces that are in league with it;

f) the plans that the problem has ready to put into action should its dominance be threatened.

Part two

Despite appearances to the contrary, problems are never totally successful in their ambitions for people's lives and relationships. However, they are usually loath to admit this and to talk openly about their failures to achieve these ambitions, which ordinarily they do their best to cover up. Therefore, when commencing to interview the problem about its failures, it is important for the investigative reporter to be acquainted with some prior knowledge of the facts of these failures. These are facts that simply cannot be denied. Because of this, in this part of the exercise, following an initial display of bravado, problems grudgingly begin to confess to these failures.

Investigative reporters have many options for questions that are effective in developing an exposé on the problem's failures. These can include an inquiry into:

a) the territories of life over which the subject still has some influence despite the problem's attempts to totally dispossess the subject;

b) the counter-techniques, counter-strategies, and the tricks that have been developed by the subject that have at times been effective in 'throwing a spanner in the works' of the problem's efforts to get the upper-hand in the subject's life;

c) the special qualities, knowledges, and skills possessed by the subject that have proven difficult for the problem to undermine and to disqualify. This can include an inquiry into the nature of the 'self-talk' that the subject has developed to challenge the problem's attempt to impose its authority on their life;

d) the purposes and commitments that guide the subject's efforts to challenge the attempts of the problem to dominate the subject's life, and that have frustrated the dreams and the hopes of the problem;

e) who stands with the subject (relatives, friends, acquaintances, teachers, therapists, and so on), and the part they have played in denying the problem's desires and wishes;

f) the options that are available to the subject for taking advantage of the problem's vulnerabilities and for the reclamation of the territories of their own life.

This exercise is demoralising of the problem, who exits from it rather dispirited. Therefore, it is important that the person who has been playing the problem does what is necessary, by way of de-roling, to break from the problem persona. It helps for this person to have the space to talk of their experience of both parts of the exercise. The person who plays the investigative reporter does not need to de-role, as this exercise opens new options for consultations that are less onerous, less weighty. It opens possibilities for a different sort of collaboration with people who seek help, and for the expression of curiosity in this work.

Part three

At this point in the exercise, the person who has been playing the subject talks of their experiences of parts 1 and 2 of the exercise. They also have the opportunity to comment on the accuracy of the portrayal of the problem. Following this, the persons who have been playing the problem and the investigative reporter talk of their experience of the first two parts of the exercise, and then all parties to the exercise are invited to share their thoughts on proposals for action that might further undermine the influence of the problem in the person's life.

Note

1. This is not referring to relationships in which abuse is being perpetrated. In these circumstances it is clearly the acts of abuse that are the problem.

References

Epston, D. & Roth, S. 1998 (in press): 'Consulting the problem about the problematic relationship: An exercise for experiencing a relationship with an externalized problem.' In Epston, D.: *Catching Up With David Epston: Published papers 1991-1996*. Adelaide: Dulwich Centre Publications. First published 1996 in Hoyt, M. (ed), *Constructive Therapies: Volume 2*. New York: Guilford.

McLean, C. 1995: 'Schools as communities of acknowledgment: A conversation with Michael White.' *Dulwich Centre Newsletter*, 2&3:51-66.

White, M. & Epston, D. 1990: *Narrative Means to Therapeutic Ends*. New York: W.W.Norton.

Notes on narrative metaphor & narrative therapy

Propositions

1. Human beings are interpreting beings - we are all active in the interpretation of, in giving meaning to, our experience as we live our lives. An act of interpretation is an achievement.

2. It is not possible for us to interpret our experience in a vacuum. A frame of intelligibility is necessary for any interpretation of lived experience.

3. Such frames provide a context for our experience, and make the attribution of meaning possible.

4. The meanings that we derive in the process of interpretation have real effects on the shape of our lives, on the steps that we take in life. Thus, such meanings are not neutral in their effects on persons' lives, but are constitutive of these lives.

5. The personal story or self-narrative provides the principal frame of intelligibility for our lived experience.

6. The personal story or self-narrative is not radically invented inside our heads. Rather, it is something that is negotiated and distributed within various communities of persons and in the institutions of our culture.

7. The personal story or self-narrative structures our experience. It is the personal story or self-narrative that determines which aspects of our stock of lived experience are selected for expression.

8. It is the personal story or self-narrative that determines the shape of the expression of particular aspects of our lived experience.

9. It is the stories that we have about our lives that actually shape or constitute our lives.

10. Our lives are multi-storied. No single story of life can be free of ambiguity and contradiction. No sole personal story or self-narrative can handle all of the contingencies of life.

11. As our lives are multi-storied, they are also multi-motived.

12. The act of living requires that we be engaged in the mediation of the dominant stories and of the sub-stories of our lives.

13. A narrative therapy is about:

   a) options for the telling and re-telling of, for the performance and re-performance of, the preferred stories of people's lives;

   b) rendering the unique, the contradictory, the contingent, and, at times, the aberrant events of people's lives significant as alternative presents;

   c) a re-engagement and a reproduction of history through the alternative presents of people's lives; a re-engagement and reproduction that brings these alternative presents together with past relevant experiences that are linked by common themes; a re-engagement and reproduction that invokes the 'wisdom of hindsight';

   d) an exploration of the alternative knowledges and skills that inform these expressions, and the identification of the cultural history and location of these skills and knowledges - these are often the subordinate knowledges and skills of culture;

   e) an exploration of the proposals for living that are associated with the particularities of action that are informed by these alternative knowledges and skills of life;

   f) thick description in that it evokes people's consciousness in explanations of why they do what they do - about the invocation of notions of desire, whim, mood, goal, hope, intention, purpose, motive, aspiration, passion, concern, value, belief, fantasy, commitment, and disposition;

g) rich description in that alternative stories of people's presents are linked with the alternative stories of people's pasts - a linking of stories across time through lives;

h) rich description in that it provides for the linking of stories between lives according to shared themes that speak to purposes, values, and commitments in common;

i) rich description in that it structures contexts for telling and re-telling, and for the re-telling of re-tellings - activities in the production of meta-texts, and texts that are meta to meta-texts;

j) processes that establish these thick or rich descriptions as the foundations for the expressions, for the performances, for the tellings that follow.

Notes on power and the culture of therapy

The culture of therapy does not have some privileged location outside of culture at large.

The culture of therapy is not exempt from the structures and ideologies of dominant culture.

The culture of therapy is not exempt from the politics of gender, race, class, age, ethnicity, heterosexism, etc.

The culture of therapy is not exempt from the politics associated with the hierarchies of knowledge and the politics of marginalisation.

Some considerations for practice

Some awareness of the extent to which the culture of therapy reproduces the dominant culture can assist us in our search for a therapeutic posture that is not wholly complicit with this. This posture can include a determination to:

a) assist persons to explore the real effects, on their lives and relationships, of some of the privileged knowledges and practices of power of dominant culture;

b) encourage persons to honour and embrace their resistance to the incitements of these dominant knowledges and practices of power;

c) privilege alternative knowledges and frames of meaning that are associated with this resistance;

d) establish the sort of structures of accountability that might expose the real and the potential abuses of power in the practices of therapy;

e) subvert the hierarchies of knowledge of the culture of psychotherapy;

f) acknowledge one's location in the social world - gender, race, class, ethnicity, sexual preference, etc. - and the various implications of this location;

g) to acknowledge the contribution of therapeutic interaction in the shaping of one's own life;

h) to consistently interview families about their experience of therapy, and about their interpretations of our motives and of our conduct;

i) to recognise and respect the fact that it is not possible for the therapeutic context to be an entirely egalitarian context, but to strive to render it more so.

Gecko

a [journal] of deconstruction [and] narrative ideas [in] therapeutic practice

FOR PEOPLE INTERESTED IN

NARRATIVE [DECONSTRUCTION] THE ETHICS OF THERAPY

'Gecko' is an exciting practice-based journal from Dulwich Centre Publications, with a focus on the ethics and practices of deconstruction and narrative therapy. It looks at the 'how' and 'why' of therapy, and aims to provide an opportunity for readers to take a fresh look at their own work through sharing in the work of others.

Subscription details for *North America*, contact:
  Dulwich Centre Publications, c/- Sarah Hughes
  PO Box 34185 Station D, Vancouver BC V6J 4N1, Canada
  ph 1888 245 4411 (toll free for North America only)

Subscription details for *Australia and elsewhere*, contact:
  Dulwich Centre Publications
  Hutt St PO Box 7192, Adelaide SA 5000, Australia
  ph (61-8) 8223 3966, fax (61-8) 8232 4441

JOURNAL

Dulwich Centre Publications' most widely read publication has changed names! The Dulwich Centre Newsletter is now titled:

Dulwich Centre Journal

This publication remains a quarterly journal which publishes creative examples of work seeking to address problems in the lives of individuals, families, and communities.

Based upon the principles which have come to be known as 'narrative ways of working', the *Dulwich Centre Journal* focuses on a wide range of issues relevant to therapy, community work, and addressing injustice.

The *Dulwich Centre Journal* offers practical examples of ways of working, while placing this work within its broader social, historical and political context.

For subscription to the *Dulwich Centre Journal,* please contact one of the following:

Australia
Dulwich Centre Publications
Hutt St PO Box 7192
Adelaide SA 5000
ph: (08) 8223 3966
fax: (08) 8232 4441

New Zealand
c/- Ann Epston
25 Queens Avenue
Balmoral, Auckland 4
ph: (09) 630 6569
fax: (09) 378 0187

North America
c/- Sarah Hughes
PO Box 34185 Station D
Vancouver BC V6J 4N1
Canada
ph* 1888 245 4411
*toll free for North America only

South Africa
c/- Dirk Kotzé
Inst. for Therapeutic Dev.
PO Box 12412
Hatfield 0028, Pretoria
South Africa
ph/fax: (12) 46 6704

Manufactured by Amazon.ca
Bolton, ON